WAR STORIES

A Memoir of Nigeria and Biafra

John Sherman

MESA VERDE PRESS

INDIANAPOLIS

Please direct inquiries to:
Mesa Verde Press
4175 Central Avenue
Indianapolis, IN 46205
mesaverdepress@earthlink.net
(317) 283-3330

First Edition

Published in the United States of America

Designed by Beyond Words, Inc.
Indianapolis

Maps created by Jim Weaver

Library of Congress Control Number: 2002105479

ISBN 0-9607220-2-5

Books by John Sherman

— Poetry —

It Give You Something To Think About (1977)
America Is A Negro Child: Race Poems
(Mesa Verde Press, 1981)
Marjorie Main: Rural Documentary Poetry
(Mesa Verde Press, 1999)

— History —

Santa Fe: A Pictorial History (Donning, 1983, 1996)
Taos: A Pictorial History (Gannon, 1990)

Acknowledgments

War Stories began as a journal kept when I was a member of a food/medical team operated by the International Committee of the Red Cross in Nigeria (1968-1969). It evolved, through several rewrites, into this memoir.

When we lived in Santa Fe, I shared the manuscript with several friends and fellow writers. Although I did the unforgivable of not writing down the names of everyone who agreed to read my work and share their thoughts with me, I know I can thank the following Santa Feans for their valuable comments: Peggy van Hulsteyn, Kathleen Christison, Bill Christison, Susan Hazen-Hammond, Orlando Romero, Peter Lawlor, Rose Mary Stearns, Bob Stearns, Elaine Pinkerton, and Carrie Vogel. If I have left anyone off of this list, I apologize for my oversight. I am also thankful to Susan Fried, Jeff Narmore, and my daughter Chizoma Sherman. Special gratitude is reserved for my wife Lois Sherman who provided valuable assistance.

Betsy Sheldon applied her editor's eye to the manuscript and gave me important feedback. I am also grateful to Karol Hovis for editing and proofreading the manuscript. The maps of Africa, Nigeria, and Biafra were skillfully produced by Jim Weaver of Indianapolis. Trish Logan of Beyond Words, Inc., used her considerable skills to design and typeset this memoir.

The poem "Surrender" was first published in *America Is A Negro Child: Race Poems*.

Introduction

This is a true story. While I did reconstruct a few direct quotes from memory, this is a recitation of actual events.

It is a personal story, a memoir of a horrific time in history. I was a Peace Corps Volunteer teacher living in the Eastern Region of Nigeria when the Region's leaders declared secession on May 30, 1967. We were, literally overnight, living in the Republic of Biafra. Six weeks later, after the civil war began, I was evacuated and spent the rest of my Peace Corps service in Malawi in southeastern Africa. More than a year after my evacuation, I returned to Nigeria and joined the International Committee of the Red Cross relief efforts. *War Stories* covers the months I worked with the Red Cross in 1968-1969, with flashbacks to my experiences as a Peace Corps Volunteer in Nigeria.

To put this memoir into perspective, I have provided, on pages i-iii, a brief chronology of events related to the history of Nigeria and Biafra from 1960 to 1970, including references to events that are discussed in this book.

The Nigerian Civil War was a great international crisis that tugged at the hearts of the world. Millions raised money, sent relief supplies, and challenged their governments to intercede in, or at least help relieve, the situation causing the deaths of so many civilians. Of particular poignancy were the stories and photos of the suffering of the children.

To many, the Nigerian Civil War (1967-1970) will seem like ancient history. To even *remember* 1967, one has to be nearly 40 years old; thus, the majority of the world's population, and perhaps the majority of the readers of this book, were born after events depicted in *War Stories*.

To those of us intimately involved, of course, the memory of Biafra will always remain a horror in our midst.

John Sherman
Indianapolis
June 2002

To the children of Nigeria and Biafra,
1967-1970

Contents

Chronology of Events
NIGERIA & BIAFRA 1960-1970

October 1960   Nigeria becomes independent from Great Britain. The country has three regions: North, West, and East. In 1963, another region (Midwest) is created.

January 1966   A military coup topples the civilian government. The coup is led by Major-General J.T.U. Aguiyi-Ironsi, an Ibo. (The largest ethnic group in the Eastern Region was the Ibo.) The coup illustrated the deep divisions in the country between the northern and southern halves. The south—composed of the Western, Midwestern, and Eastern Regions—was predominately Christian while the vast Northern Region, comprising more than half the country, was predominately Muslim.

During the first six years of independence, religious differences, political factions, a disparity in educational opportunities, and economic difficulties in many areas of the country led to great dissatisfaction with the civilian government.

June 1966   *I enter Peace Corps training for Nigeria, to become an English teacher in the Eastern Region; the training is held at the Atlanta University complex in Atlanta, Georgia.*

July 1966	A second military coup, led by Lt.-Col. (later General) Yakubu Gowon, topples the first military government. Ironsi is killed. Although Gowon was from the Northern Region, he was a Christian. Ironsi had attempted to make many changes in the fundamental governing of the country; that, along with a long-held distrust of the Ibos by many from the Northern Region, encouraged Gowon and others to act.
September 1966	*I arrive in Nigeria to begin service as a Peace Corps Volunteer in the Eastern Region.*
October 1966	A pogrom occurs in the Northern Region, in which thousands of Ibos are killed, mostly by civilians. The Ibos had held many jobs in the civil service and in such areas as banking, to the resentment of the Northerners; many survivors flee home to the Eastern Region. Northerners living in the Eastern Region are killed in retaliation. *De facto* secession occurs, and little travel takes place between the regions.
May 1967	After months of talk about secession, and an increase in tensions, the Eastern Region secedes and is named the Republic of Biafra. (The Bight of Biafra is a body of water off the coast of Nigeria in the Atlantic Ocean.) Eventually, four countries recognize Biafra, but the rest of the world continues to respect the sovereignty of Nigeria.
July 1967	War breaks out when Nigerian troops invade Biafra.
	Schools in the Eastern Region close and the students are sent home. Peace Corps Volunteers and other expatriates are evacuated from Biafra. I am reassigned to Malawi in southeastern Africa.

PERIOD OF TIME
COVERED BY "WAR STORIES"

August 1968   *I return to Nigeria. I get hired by the Red Cross to help with the relief efforts, first in Lagos, then in Elele, a village in the Eastern Region (in a part of the former Biafra that is back in Nigerian hands).*

By August 1968, in the 13th month of the war, Biafra has shrunk to about half of its original size. The borders between Nigeria and Biafra shift, but do not change much, between August 1968 and April 1969.

By the time I return to Nigeria, the world has become acutely aware of the toll the war is taking on the civilians, particularly on the children within Biafra. As a result, relief efforts, supported by many individuals, organizations, and governments, have been organized to aid persons on both sides of the front lines. Even though suffering is rampant on the Nigerian side of the war, most of the rest of the world believes the crisis is within the Biafran borders only.

April 1969   *I leave Nigeria and return to the United States.*

January 1970   Biafra surrenders and is reincorporated into Nigeria. Hundreds of thousands, perhaps millions, of soldiers and civilians have died; many others suffer physical and psychological damage.

Glossary

3d	*three pence*
6d	*six pence*
agbada	*loose-fitting garment*
Beke	*white person (Pidgin English)*
dash	*gift, tip, extra portion, bribe*
groundnuts	*peanuts*
High Life	*popular, non-traditional style of dancing*
Ibo	*refers to the ethnic group*
Igbo	*refers to the language spoken by Ibo people*
ki-ki bus	*small bus used for public transportation*
kwashiorkor	*severe protein malnutrition—recognizable by lethargy, depigmentation of the skin, loss of hair or change in hair color, etc.—that was found in many children on both sides of the civil war*
lorry	*truck*
motor park	*a transportation center where one went to obtain a ride in a lorry or a taxi*
onye ocha	*white person (Igbo)*
onye ogi	*black person (Igbo)*
pekin	*small child (Pidgin English)*
Pidgin English	*lingua franca in Nigeria, especially coastal area*

Map of Africa

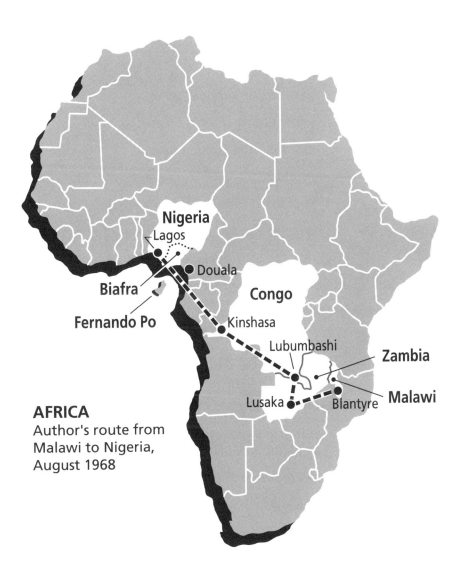

Nigeria
Lagos
Douala
Biafra
Congo
Fernando Po
Kinshasa
Lubumbashi
Zambia
Lusaka
Malawi
Blantyre

AFRICA
Author's route from
Malawi to Nigeria,
August 1968

Map of Nigeria

NIGERIA
Original Biafran borders (dotted line)
are identical to those of the Eastern Region of
Nigeria at the onset of secession on May 30, 1967

MAP OF BIAFRA

BIAFRA
Outer border shows original size of Biafra at secession.
White area shows what remained of Biafra during time
covered in this book (August 1968–April 1969).
Borders are approximate. Certain localities, such as the city
of Owerri, changed hands between the Nigerians and
the Biafrans more than once during the war.

AUGUST 1968 – LAGOS

My heart begins to beat fast whenever I think of what I am about to do.

I have to look away from everyone and stare at the rust on the roof or at the lizards running along the tarmac in front of the airport building.

The man in front of me turns around, suddenly.

"Sorry! Didn't mean to startle you. Beastly queue." He looks to see who might be listening. "Wonder these chaps can get us through at all, isn't it." He frowns and shakes his head as if he has bitten into something distasteful.

"These soldiers!" he adds. "They pick the biggest ones they can find for customs duty, but they never think to pick the smartest ones, now, do they?" He doesn't expect a reply, and I give none, other than a sympathetic nod.

I hold my blue entry card in one hand, a newspaper over my head to give me some small comfort from the sun, and stare at the dozen men, all white, all older than I am by a generation, who stand between the ugly gray building and me.

Just then the line moves. The man is looking back at the plane. "The queue," I say. He turns around and adjusts the strap of his shoulder bag. Those ahead of us are reaching down and scooting their hand luggage along with them.

Barbara is just inside the door. She looks my way two or three times, but I avoid her gaze. We agreed on the Pan Am flight not to go in together.

✤ ✤ ✤

When I first mentioned separating once we were off the plane, she had said, "I don't mind staying together," but I shook my head.

"No, if I get caught, I don't want you involved. It's only one of those crazy coincidences that we ended up on this same flight anyway."

"Where did you stay last night?" she asked.

"At the Hotel du Port. Kinshasa's finest."

"I tried to get in there. My flight got in too late. I was at the Palais." She began to brush her hair.

"Do you really think you'll get caught over something like that?" She pointed to my blue entry card.

I took a breath. Then I shrugged and made what I hoped was a happy-go-lucky, wry kind of smile. "Oh, I don't know. I doubt it."

"How long will you be in Lagos?"

"Three days," I said. I patted my shoulder bag. "I've got a ticket to Douala." I lowered my voice although probably no one could hear me over the cabin noise. "From there, it's only a hop over to Fernando Po. And then"—I 'flew' my hand—"right back into Biafra on one of the Red Cross flights."

"Did you fly to Kinshasa from Malawi?"

"No, from Zambia," I said, with a heavy sigh. "I got stuck in Lusaka for a whole week. I missed the weekly flight to Congo by two hours."

"Lusaka! For a week! Sorry!"

"That's what I said when I found out. It drove me crazy to be there for that long when I was trying to get back here. Two hours!" I laughed.

"What's so funny?"

"Something did happen last night that was funny, in the middle of all this craziness. All last week, I kept going into the airline office in downtown Lusaka to check on my flight, just to see if anything had changed. I must have been their most faithful customer—or their most irritating." I took a sip of my drink.

"When I got to the Lusaka airport last night, I discovered that they had overbooked the flight by a lot of people. A *lot* of people! We were all determined to get on the plane. Can you imagine waiting another week? I made it on, but then they announced that all the men had to get back off. I got off. We stood on the tarmac, muttering. Then they said that all the men who had wives on board could get on the plane. That still left several of us. The airline guy who was making all these pronouncements was the very guy that had waited on me, every day, at the office. He looked at the rest of us, spotted me, and jerked his thumb towards the airplane's stairs. 'You!' he shouted. 'Get on board.'"

We laughed together. The stewardess, walking down the aisle, smiled at us.

I leaned back. The journey seemed almost over, and yet it seemed as if it would never, never end.

"I'll be in Lagos three days, too," she said. "Then I fly out for New York."

"Are you glad to be going back?"

"Home?"

"No, Lagos."

"I'll be glad to see my friends. But, Lagos? No thanks." She let down her tray table and placed her blue card on it. "Now, look," she said, playing with her pencil, "what if they have some kind of records at the airport on Peace Corps Volunteers who lived in Biafra? Or expatriates who've flown out of Lagos since the war began? Or—" She shrugged her shoulders, then frowned. "Are you sure you want to do it this way?"

"Sure," I grinned. "I know I don't want to pull what you're doing."

She grinned back. She showed me her blue card again. "Don't you think this'll work?"

"Until they ask you to clarify that funny little pencil mark. Then you'll have to let them know whether you meant to check the 'Yes' or the 'No.'"

"I'll say 'No' if that happens. And then we'll be in the same boat."

"Or the same army lorry heading for prison."

We sat a while, listening to the gradual descent of the plane. We were still in the clouds.

"Did you like this past year in Malawi?" she asked.

"Ummm. I liked my students. I always like my students. But I kept thinking and kept thinking of Biafra. All those awful pictures. It haunted me all year."

"I know what you mean. I did the same thing."

"And now I'll be there in a matter of days," I said. It seemed impossible.

"I wonder how many have died?" she asked.

I didn't answer. We busied ourselves with the rest of the questions on our blue cards.

✤   ✤   ✤

I am now six people from the door and I can see more clearly the Nigerian Customs men in their brown uniforms and caps with visors. And the inevitable dark glasses. Whether they are really Customs men or just army men filling in, I don't know. And I decide it doesn't matter. An orange-headed lizard startles me by coming close to my bag. I don't see it until I reach down to move the bag along in the line. The lizard is doing "push-ups," its dinosaur-like head bobbing up and down. I jerk back, terrifying it in the process, and then move forward towards the door.

Behind me are a half-dozen other passengers. Only one of them is black. He looks like a Nigerian. How he can stand to be dressed in a Western suit and tie in this sun, I don't know. I am wearing a cotton shirt and pants and I am dying to get to a shower and an air-conditioned room.

✤   ✤   ✤

My first minute in Africa began with a gasp nearly two years ago when it was my turn to step out of the chartered flight from New York into the humidity of Lagos. "Oh, Christ," said another Volunteer in front of me, "and it's only five a.m. What'll it be like by noon?"

The humidity gathered, collected, exhaled from the cement buildings.

Lizards. Palm trees. Tall, rich-dark chocolate people with the strong accents in English we knew from our Nigerian trainers in Atlanta.

We were exultant. We were depressed. Our clothes were soaked through. High Life music blared from somebody's radio, somewhere. One, then two, of us started to dance. The customs people clapped their hands, called out in rapid Pidgin English to their fellow workers to look at us, then all of us laughed.

Nigeria!

✛ ✛ ✛

I feel for my papers for what must be the dozenth time since leaving the plane. The passport is new. The one I used to have, the Peace Corps-issued one with visas from Nigeria and Biafra, is now surrendered. It's probably still in our embassy in Malawi.

The health card is also new. It hadn't expired, but I knew I had to get rid of everything that tied me to Nigeria or Biafra. A sympathetic American nurse helped me concoct this one. The shots, which I really received in Nigeria, are now shown to have been given to me in Malawi. The old card told the truth.

And then there's the blue card. All the information is accurate except for one item. "Have you ever been to Nigeria before?" it says. A very simple question. One that can be answered with a check mark in a 'Yes' box or a 'No' box. And I have placed a bold, black pen mark in the 'No' box.

I am afraid that if I say 'Yes' I will have to reveal where I lived and when I lived there, and I will be ushered out of the country on another flight today. Or detained. These people are sensitive. They are dying just like the Biafrans, but not so quickly. Or so publicly.

✛ ✛ ✛

Our lorry driver seemed only to have two items for driving: a horn and an accelerator. He accompanied them with shouts, loud laughter, the shaking of fists, more laughter and a frightening propensity to carry on conversations with other lorry drivers while their vehicles were barreling down the same narrow street crowded on both sides by hundreds of pedestrians poised to hurl themselves across, if the traffic ever cleared. We could only laugh. One of the Volunteers shouted, "Welcome to Nigeria!"

The driver immediately cried out, "Yes! Welcome, my friends, welcome na Lagos!" he shouted to us. "Yes, welcome!" He beat on the steering wheel. "Lagos be my home. Where be you going, my friends?" When we shouted that we were going to the Eastern

Region, he scowled. "That be Ibo land." He shook his head. "Ibos. Not good," he said. He blew his horn at a woman who dared try to cross in front of his lorry. He made a scolding sound, sort of a sucking in of air. "Bad woman!" he shouted. "Bad woman!"

✛ ✛ ✛

What a crazy war. No one even seems sure of the front lines anymore, or so the international press tells us. Every map I see does, however, show a Biafra that is shrinking by the week. Port Harcourt, my old stomping grounds and once a major city in Biafra, is now again a major city in Nigeria. Imagine. So many places are like P.H.—they've gone from Nigerian to Biafran to Nigerian once again. Military schizophrenia.

✛ ✛ ✛

In Lusaka, on the journey here from Malawi, I was disturbed to see the group of military symbols on display in the Anglican cathedral. The whites living in Zambia were honoring their own, I guessed. They had placed these shields at the entrance to a memorial chapel within the cathedral. World War II seemed distant, dry history.

It struck me: When would Nigeria's and Biafra's current events become so distant and so dry?

I lowered myself into a pew at the back and bowed my head. I did not form words, but only surged forth with feeling, and grasped at my own phrases bouncing about. Would I make it to Biafra? Yes, God, let me. Would I be able to do anything? Yes, God.... Would Biafra survive? Yes, yes, God!

Now, days later, near the end of my journey from the gentle mountains of Malawi to the sure hysteria of Biafra, I recall that I did not ask for my own survival.

As I knelt in that pew, a group of whites came suddenly through a side door. They were noisy, laughing, full of Saturday-morning cheer. The frenzied preparations for a church bazaar occupied their minds, and the loud laughter bounced around the cathedral walls. No one seemed to realize I was there. When it was obvious they were going to be working there the rest of the morning, I got up and left. On my way out, I felt the metal shields identifying the various military units. They had sharp edges and were cold to the touch.

✦ ✦ ✦

I have been quoted in the American press as saying, "Biafra deserves to win." That phrase comes back to me again, as it did on the plane, as it did when I first got in this line, as it did only a few minutes ago, when I spied the tall, mean-looking Customs man talking angrily to a white man cowering in front of him.

Biafra's chances, at this point, are hard to predict. I cannot separate my desire for Biafra to win from the reality of the military situation. Biafra has lost much of its land. Port Harcourt, Enugu, Calabar—all of these cities are back in Nigerian hands. There are no ports, no coast of any kind, and food and guns have to be flown in, over Nigerian territory. I expect to be on one of those planes, flying in from Fernando Po, the island off the coast that has the airfield used by both the Red Cross and the gun runners.

Biafra can win. It must win. It does deserve to win. And here I am, thinking those thoughts, standing in the capital of the country that is determined that it, not Biafra, will win, pretending that I am simply passing through on an innocent mission. But it *is* an innocent mission, although no one here would believe that.

✦ ✦ ✦

Have I lived in Nigeria before? Yes, sir, I have lived here. I have taught your children, eaten your peppery food, watched you prepare for war, seen a bomb shelter being dug outside my window, observed my students march with sticks on their shoulders, and sailed down the Bonny river away from Port Harcourt and out of Biafra. And that was only last year, and yet it was a lifetime ago. My lifetime. I have spent the past year in the quietness of Malawi, clear across the continent, reading about the tragedy of Biafra until I decided one day while listening to Chopin that I couldn't bear just reading, and I went to the headmaster and quit. "I'm going back to Biafra," I said. Just like that. Even then, just a few weeks back, seems so long ago. I begin to wonder all over again if this journey to Biafra will ever end. I have been in too many countries, too many airline offices, too many consulates getting visas, too many ugly hotel rooms in the past three weeks. And now I am standing here, trying to appear calm, but scared to death, waiting to go inside and present my lie to the Customs men and hoping they fall for it.

For the first time in my life, a war is so overpoweringly personal. I *know* so many of these people. They are former students and their families, former fellow teachers, the guy who helped me climb into the bus on the way to Port Harcourt on Saturday mornings, and the woman who sold me groundnuts at the motor park. Names. Faces. Histories.

Listening to Chopin, the desire to do *something* overwhelmed me. I could drive a lorry for the Red Cross. I could wrap bandages. I could spoon feed a child. Something. I must do something.

✤ ✤ ✤

The mattresses at the University of Lagos were damp. The newspaper, the writing tablet, the aerogrammes—all were limp. My kingdom for an air conditioner. Stories abounded from Volunteers who showed up to welcome us to Nigeria. Stories about snakes, and mold and mildew, and teaching kids who only wanted to learn, by rote, what was on the exams, intolerant of attempts to share the joys of learning. Some fellow new Volunteers looked worried. Walking to the campus dining hall, we took turns watching for snakes. Some looked in the grass, others in the trees. The nights were hot, horribly hot. And the mattresses smelled of mildew.

✤ ✤ ✤

My turn is next. I am sweating too much. Some of it comes from the sun. Some of it comes from knowing I am going to show them a crisp blue card with a lie on it. Suppose they find out it's a lie, suppose somehow they find out, and then they look at my ticket, which shows I'm to fly out of here in three days for the Cameroons, and one of them, smarter than the rest, puts two and two together and says: He's going to Douala. That's in the Cameroons. That's so he can go from there to Fernando Po so he can get—and suddenly you see everyone catching on—to Biafra! Then they will all think out loud: Why did he come to Nigeria? He's a spy. Yes, he's a spy, someone will shout, and others will come running, the kind of people who always come running when others shout. And I will stand there, shaking my head and bobbing my Adam's apple and wonder what—

"Next! Come, come, hurry, hurry!"

I hand in my passport. "Bring your entry card."

I hand it to him. I hand in my health card, too, but he shoves it rudely back at me.

My shirt is very wet. I push back some hair that insists on lying on my forehead. I can feel sweat running down my chest. It almost tickles. I want to laugh.

He is tall, very tall, and extremely black. I can see the careful scarification on his face. He is, I am sure, from the North, the area of the country most opposed to Biafra. He has an assistant in civilian clothes. I am amazed at how angry they look. I want to make small talk, smile, speak about the weather, or the lizards outside, or the civilian man's embroidered shirt, or about men who sneak into other men's countries with faked papers on their way to enemy territory.

The soldier is carefully looking at my passport, searching each page slowly. I am telling myself, *Be calm, be calm.* He comes to the Nigerian visa.

"Where did you get this?" He almost shouts it.

"Blantyre."

"Huh!? Where?"

"Malawi."

"Mali."

"No, Malawi. Central Africa."

My Adam's apple moves again. I am trying to keep in control, but I feel almost as if I am going to faint. I can see Barbara waiting for someone to look through her luggage. She does not look my way.

Biafra deserves to win. Biafra deserves to win.

Why did I ever say that? I am sure that this man standing in front of me, now looking over my entry card, has never seen the little Indiana newspaper that quote appeared in, and I am almost relieved, then very relieved.

But, when I think about clipping services and how it is probable that the Nigerian Embassy in Washington has such a service and the article could have been found and is now somewhere in that desk in front of me, I take a breath and blow hot air out of my mouth. No, that's not possible, I think. Yes, that's possible, I think.

Biafra deserves to win.

If I am caught and dragged away, I'll shout it at them all.

"Where are you lodging in Lagos?"

I had anticipated that question, at least. "At the Bristol Hotel."

He nods. He knows the hotel. I thought I should have the name of a hotel, or else it might cause some kind of trouble. I asked another American, a businessman, at the Hotel du Port last night. If I am asked, I shall say I have reservations. That will also be a lie.

Suddenly, he is saying something else to me, something I can't believe he is saying: "Have you ever been to Nigeria before?"

"No." No elaboration. No need to say anything else. Go on, go on.

"No?" he asks. He gives me that angry frown again. Is he then smiling, or is that a kind of sarcastic grimace he is making?

"No," I say. I am staring right back at him, not smiling, not frowning. I am simply giving him a clear answer. I hate my Adam's apple. I am afraid it suggests deceit.

He reaches for a stack of cards I had not seen and begins to look through them, every so often looking back at my name on the form and then back at the cards. I feel numb. This may be a list of people evacuated from Biafra after the war began, a list with my name on it. It could be a list of Peace Corps Volunteers. It could be a list of people whose support of Biafra has appeared in print. It could have my name on it.

The assistant waits until he has finished, and then he looks at me. He frowns. "Are you sure you haven't been to Nigeria before?"

I give him a very, very slight smile. "Yes, I'm sure. I've not been here before."

The assistant reaches for another stack of cards. The soldier adjusts the rifle resting against the counter. The assistant is more efficient, but he too looks over at my passport every so many cards.

Finally, he stops. He pushes the passport at the soldier, who takes it, turns to the page with the Nigerian visa, and stamps it, then puts a scrawl on his stamp. He hands me the passport and the blue card, then takes back the card. "Move on," he says, suddenly impatient to be rid of me.

I walk away, truly expecting to hear "Come!" from one of them. I get in line for the health inspection. I now worry that the woman, used to seeing so many health cards, will be suspicious that such a new card has items more than two years old on it. My excuse is that the other one was lost, but my embassy had records of my shots. What if she puzzles over this too loudly, and the civilian back at Customs hears her and decides this is all very interesting?

The woman is bored. She takes my health card, flips through it with obvious disgust, and barks at me, "Blood type!" She shoves the card at me, almost knocking it off my side of the counter onto the floor, and I fill in the information I had left out. She has barely looked at the entries we so carefully manufactured.

I stand there after I am done, afraid to leave without permission, and she shakes her head again in disgust. "Finish!" she says, and reaches out her hand for the card of the man behind me.

My suitcase I do not worry about. There is nothing there that can incriminate me. Last night in Kinshasa I went over everything, throwing out two shirts that came from West Africa, searching through my papers in my billfold for anything that might link me with a previous life in Nigeria, or even a visit, or with the Peace Corps, so today some Congolese man in Kinshasa is walking around with a Nigerian shirt on, and wondering why the white man in the hotel room left it and another one there, along with a tiny pile of torn-up papers. The pieces were so small I was sure no one could glue them together.

The baggage inspector raises his fat leg and places it on the counter behind my bag. He reaches over and looks through my belongings. He yawns a few times, and slaps at insects flying around his thick neck. Only once does he stop as he goes through my things. "How many these you bring?" he asks, pointing to a pack of cigarettes.

"Eight," I say. I know it's under the limit. He looks as if he really doesn't believe me, but he's not going to bother to count all the packs I have there. I am waiting for him to ask for one of them, but he doesn't.

Suddenly, I am free. I hurry out of the building, after showing my papers yet one more time. The man guarding the exit flips through them so quickly he couldn't have read a thing.

Outside, Barbara is waiting amid a throng of taxi drivers. She and I embrace. She too is wet. I say unnecessarily, "It's OK."

We bargain for the taxi ride into the city. On the way, I give her cryptic comments about what took place, glancing often at the back of the driver's head.

She gets out at her friends' house in the suburbs. "Good luck," she says, and hugs me again. "I'll come see you tomorrow at the Bristol."

I face Lagos alone. I am stunned by what I see. I had felt that returning to West Africa after only a little more than a year's absence was merely to return home, but now I am overcome by the noise, the dirt, the excitement of the slums of Lagos. I spy naked children running about and remind myself that that is common here, while in Malawi it is not. Women hurry back and forth, sometimes running dangerously close to the cars that blow their horns at them. The women are dressed in cloth of wild colors and patterns, with pans of enormous quantities of things on their heads. Men piss in the open sewers. The smell of those sewers brings back Port Harcourt and Benin City and Enugu and Lagos, and I smile slightly. It reminds me of this country that is trying to stay together or trying to keep itself apart, whichever side you choose.

I feel as if I am now on a journey through an allegorical novel. I am protected from the environment because I am behind the door of a taxi, yet I am a part of it because children run up to my window and shout *"Beke!"* or "White man, dash me penny!" I smile at them, now so relieved to be where I am, and they giggle or scream and rush back to their mothers and the other children. Rapid conversations, shouts, more laughter.

Everything is colorful: the women's clothing, the buildings in faded pastels, the signboards, the big metal pans. Everything is noise: the taxi horns; the people shouting, laughing and selling; the records being blasted from the shops; the children's shrill voices calling to one another.

I lean back in my seat, overcome by the heat, the humidity, the airport ordeal, the idea that I am at last back in Nigeria, and by everything that I am seeing from my cracked window.

✦   ✦   ✦

We exited the taxi, glad to be at the High Life club, gladder to be out of the mad rush of automobiles, led at times by our own taxi driver. *"I thought we were going to die when he passed that other taxi!" whispered one friend.*

We made a run into the club to get out of the rain, only to discover that the club had no roof. Laughter, while we huddled along a wall, trying futilely to keep dry. Soon, the rain stopped, the big, already-familiar green bottles of Star beer arrived, the music continued. We had learned how to dance the High Life in Peace Corps training. I was one of the bold ones, heading for the dance floor while still sober. Four of us began dancing and the place erupted in applause and shouts. A man ran over to me. "Where you learn High Life?" he asked, grasping my hand. "America!" I shouted. "Wondaful!" he replied. He turned to the crowd at our end of the dance floor. "America!" he shouted. "Wondaful!"

+ + +

There is a room at the Bristol, so I am spared from getting another taxi to a second hotel. It is raining hard. Once I am alone, I strip and walk into the bathroom. The shower, first hot, then cool, then cold, brings me back to life. I wash my hair, brush my teeth, do everything I can to come alive. The room is almost too cold.

+ + +

In the dining hall, we were served American corn flakes with warm, sweet, thick milk. "Oh, gag," a friend said, "I think I'm going to throw up."

We bought groundnuts on the street from a vendor. First, he rolled them roughly in his hand to get rid of the paper-thin shells, then he tossed them up in the air and blew the shells away. "I don't think I want any," the same friend said. Then the vendor took a piece of newspaper, rolled it into the shape of an ice-cream cone and poured the nuts into it. They tasted marvelous. "Want some?" I asked my friend. He shook his head.

+ + +

Soon, I am at the bar downstairs where I give an order I have wanted to place for more than a year. "Star beer," I say, and break into a grin. I take a sip, realize it is far too cold, and let it rest. I read about the war in the *Time* I have just bought, and the bartender joins me. He clucks his tongue. "This war," he says. "Too much!"

I am smoking constantly, and munching on groundnuts from a dish before me. He has filled it three times. I finish my beer before I go in to have dinner.

I choose the European side of the menu, which here means British. Dinner begins with oxtail soup. The food is pleasant enough, but when I am just beginning the main course, I start to feel sick. I can tell it will not go away.

I rise and the waiter hurries over. "I am ill," I say.

He has a panicked look. "You must still pay for the dinner," he says. I nod. I only want to leave. I quickly sign my check and hurry out. I barely make it to my room in time.

I spend the rest of the night throwing up again and again and again.

SEPTEMBER 1968 – LAGOS

It is quiet in the house.

I am restless. I sit at the table smoking one cigarette after another, wondering why I can't just go to bed like everyone else.

✛   ✛   ✛

We were among Ibos at last. Thousands of Ibos—and others—filled the market at Onitsha. I had never experienced such a mass of humanity. Children and women carried immense loads on their heads, the weight separated from their skulls only by a rolled-up rag. How did they do it? Everyone was bargaining, shouting and laughing in the process. We had been warned: Watch your money. If you don't bargain, they won't respect you. Be prepared to be cheated. My eyes must have been wide open. How tame was anything else in my experience! The word was: You can buy anything you want at the Onitsha Market. A story: A European man driving an unusual vehicle went to a car-parts vendor in the market, seeking to replace one of his side mirrors. Minutes later, he was astounded to be brought exactly what he needed. After he had wended his way out of the market to his vehicle, he discovered his other side mirror was missing. He had just purchased it.

We had arrived in Eastern Nigeria—"the East"—days before on a bumpy flight from Lagos. Since the concentration of our Peace Corps training had been on this region of the country, we, at last, felt we had reached our destination. "The East, the East," our Ibo teachers had said with proud smiles. "Home."

✦ ✦ ✦

I almost drop my corner of the stretcher because the man jerks so violently and cries out.

The others who have traveled with him from Port Harcourt to Lagos must have known he might do that, but his sudden spasm of pain surprises me.

I don't think it is the man's movements that make me almost drop the stretcher. I think it is the horridness of his crying out. It isn't the sort of made-for-television crying that you expect, even though you have been warned that real pain doesn't come in such tones of agony. It is the guttural, slurred, gurgling-sounding noise that seems almost to be in my ear, although I am carrying a corner where his feet are. At least this one has feet.

That must be why I am sitting here, staring at the wall, not even wanting a beer, although it is incredibly hot and humid down here in the living room where we don't have air conditioning. I count the butts in this ashtray and come up with 15. I realize that not all of them are mine.

A few belong to Charlie, who is with Save the Children. He teases me about being with the International Committee of the Red Cross.

It's usually just referred to as "the ICRC." ("The Irk-cee," says Charlie. "They should all go back to Switzerland.") No one here likes the ICRC. The Nigerian press reflects the Nigerian government belief that the Red Cross, indeed the whole relief effort, is designed to thwart the Nigerian army's efforts to win this war swiftly and efficiently. Most Nigerians can't fathom, either, how the ICRC or any of the other relief groups can have people working on both sides of the war. They think of the relief workers inside Biafra as their enemies.

There are charges made by the press constantly that even the relief workers on this side are responsible for feeding civilians who pass the food to Biafran soldiers, thus sustaining the war. When I was in Kingsway yesterday, one of the clerks asked me where I worked. I learn fast. "At a company down on the Marina," I said.

"Which company?"

"Shell-BP."

"My cousin needs a job. Can you get him one with Shell-BP?"

I said no. It was an honest answer.

The other organizations mostly feel that the ICRC is not the best one to be in charge of this whole operation. "They keep screwing up!" yells Charlie, or Bill (OXFAM), or Theo (UNICEF) at least once a night when they come back to our common living quarters, this yellow house in a very fine neighborhood. I am, at least, never blamed for any of the messes caused by the ICRC. It is the Swiss bureaucrats sitting in the Lagos office—or the Geneva headquarters—who are the subjects of all this venom.

I wonder what I would be doing tonight if I had made it into Biafra. I might be sitting calmly having a cigarette in Owerri or Aba or some Ibo village. I can't imagine what I would have done if I had kept my original itinerary and gone on to Douala and then to Fernando Po—and then found out I couldn't get into Biafra.

+ + +

I had never seen a Catholic priest in a T-shirt and shorts. I was amused. He was tall and thin, with graying temples and steel-wire glasses. "Glad to have you," he said in his Southern accent. I had been told they were Benedictine monks from Arkansas. "Surely you jest," I had said to the Peace Corps official who assured me that he wasn't. Arkansas?! Here, in the middle of West Africa, I was doomed to work with monks from the American South. Little Rock. Central High School. Lord!

We traveled south from Enugu towards my new life, on a school compound in Eleme, 17 miles from Port Harcourt.

We drove up the long lane. School had begun. Students in white uniforms were cutting the grass with machetes or shaking cleaning rags off the second-floor balcony of the main building. Suddenly, I was terrified. All this time, it had been in the future: After you finish college.... After you finish Peace Corps training.... After you get to Nigeria.... After you get to Enugu.... This was the "after." Visions of other black students, guarded by bayonets, clouded my mind.

✚　✚　✚

One day after our arrival in Lagos, Barbara told me what her friends said: "You have absolutely no chance of getting into Biafra now that you've been in Nigeria."

"But—" I wanted to hit her. Kill the messenger who brings bad news.

"They said that if you've got a Nigerian visa, the Biafrans won't have anything to do with you." She looked around the hotel dining room. "Now what?"

I felt trapped, suffocated after my long journey.

I spotted a van with the words "International Committee of the Red Cross (I.C.R.C.)" on it as I waited under an awning for the heavy rains to stop. I was not aware the Red Cross was working on this side of the war.

I met with a Dr. Bulle, an American with a thick accent of some kind, and he hired me in less than five minutes. He was most impressed that I had been here before. "There are too many greenhorns here," he said in disgust. "You'll find out for yourself."

I looked puzzled. He laid his pipe on the desk. "The Swiss! Ha!" He narrowed his eyes. "They are escaping dull work, dull marriages and the staleness of Switzerland." He seemed to spit out the words, as if they themselves were guilty of staleness. "And," he said, "many of them do not even speak English! How can they expect to deal with Nigerians, I ask you?"

Bulle is always angry. I see him going up and down the stairs at the ICRC headquarters when I stop there on my way to the airport each morning. He will smile at me, and often ask how I am; then, before we have both gone on our way, he gets that scowl on his face again. I think he'll chew the pipe stem in two if he's not careful.

What he said about the Swiss is true, only he didn't even mention their racism. Nor their interest in the numbers I can provide for their charts. Their obsession with those numbers. How many tons of food. How many people were fed. How many people were treated. How many this. How many that. Numbers. Numbers. Numbers!

I am convinced the lack of planning of the ICRC is an extension of their racism. If a tragedy of this magnitude were happening in Europe right now, they would be so horrified they'd have it well planned and coordinated; as it is, they blame their own faults on the humidity, or on the fact they're in West Africa, or on the Nigerians. Sometimes, they're right; most of the time, they're not.

✦ ✦ ✦

The students stood up when they answered questions. "Sah!" they cried out, waving their hands, seeking my attention. I was knee deep in verbs one hour and sentence-structure drills the next. I returned to my house for lunch served by Godfrey, a steward who cooked, cleaned and shopped in the market for me, and then it was back again to the classrooms. I was enthralled with teaching, shaking with emotion on days when I saw them understand and frustrated with emotion on days they did not.

✦ ✦ ✦

We are continually discussing food. Monty, who was a lorry driver in England and who is embarrassed as hell to be stuck in a house with several college graduates, talks about it the most. We have long discussions about the fish, or about ways to prepare potatoes. He is the only one of us who cannot seem to get by a day without grousing at the two stewards who cook and clean for us. "Simon!" he'll call in that awful bark of his. "Make some fresh coffee! This is bloody awful!" I raise my eyebrows at Simon, behind Monty's back, and Simon is hard put to keep from breaking out into a grin. I decide I'd better not do that again or Monty will take it out on Simon when no one is around to defend him.

If we're not discussing food, we're going over the intricacies of British English versus American English. "You don't sound like an American," they say, and I tell them that, after two years in former British colonies teaching British English, I never fail to use "lorry" for "truck," or "torch" for "flashlight," or "petrol" for "gasoline." We have a good laugh: One of them asks me what the Americanism is for the bonnet of an automobile, and I can't remember. "Why, why, it's…it's…bloody hell!" I say, and we roar.

✦ ✦ ✦

The students leaned forward. I pronounced the words from the lesson not as a Hoosier but as an Englishman. "La-BOR-uh-

tree," I said for that room used in chemistry class. I puzzled about our differences, the English and the Americans.

There was trouble in the North. Tension between the Ibos and the Northerners. The local government radio stations and the local newspapers haven't a shred of objectivity, not even a pretense. They refer to the Northerners as "vandals," and write and speak of "strangers," ominous creatures we are to be frightened of. We are good; they are bad. And the students and teachers believe every word they read. Might all of us writers have such power!

✛ ✛ ✛

"Plane dey come!" Emmanuel calls. I am sitting on a stack of boxes in our end-of-runway warehouse.

"Come! Come! Make you come!" he cries to his men. One of the DC-4s is heading our way, splashing water high into the air on both sides. We are enduring heavy rains these days. All of us jump up and begin to count out the pallets that will go on this flight. I reach for my inventory sheets tucked neatly under the clamp of the Red Cross-issued clipboard.

Emmanuel walks over to the forklift and starts the motor. "Which?" he asks. He points to the pallets. He slips the long black forks into a pallet, lifts it up, and heads onto the tarmac. The plane pulls up towards us, then turns around, and we duck from the draft and the putrid smell of its petrol. Some loose papers blow further back into the building. The cargo door opens. It's Smitty. I wonder if I have ever seen him without a cigarette.

"Calabar! We're goin' to Calabar!" I nod. "Did Bucks go to Port Harcourt yet?" I nod again, and shout "Yes!" although I don't think he can hear me. After the engines are shut off, it takes us only a few minutes to load our usual ten tons.

When they are ready to take off, I stand too close and the propellers blow sand into my eyes.

They are coming so often now. Three planeloads of wounded today so far. I wonder if they bring back the dead ones, or if they leave them there. I do know that you have to bury them quickly here. Bury *us* quickly here.

✛ ✛ ✛

I can't see any damage from the bomb the Biafrans dropped on the office building along the Lagos Marina. No one was killed, but the noise terrified those nearby. I open the side door of the Anglican cathedral and find a pew. The brilliant sunlight pours through the windows.

I am telling God a few things when one of the Nigerian clergy comes in with a couple.

"I will be standing here when you come up to the altar," he says to them, and I guess there is to be a wedding. When he brings them back to the pew where I am kneeling, he smiles down at me and says, "So sorry. This won't take long."

I nod but I am annoyed. They spend a lot of time talking about all sorts of trivia, and I finally leave before they do.

✦ ✦ ✦

The radio commentator spoke of de facto *secession. "Secession" was a word used more and more since The Troubles in the North. Ibos did not travel to the North any more; Northerners—live ones, anyway—were not found in the East. I felt claustrophobic.*

✦ ✦ ✦

I can stay up because I'm younger and need less sleep, I suppose, and I can stare at the wall and think, something I seem to have done a tremendous amount of lately. I want to cry, to vent my feelings, but I can get no tears to come. It puzzles me.

Red blood looks so dramatic against black skin. On white bandages, it's diffused, soaked in, and one gets used to the color, as if the bandages are supposed to be pinkish-red. But smack against their skin, it stands out in a way that I don't expect it to. A bubble of blood just getting itself ready to harden is bright, wet and very red, and, against the deep, deep brown background, it has an eerie beauty to it. I have the feeling that I should not appreciate it quite so much, that I should be ashamed at even the thought of such an appreciation. Yet it draws me to it, as I am drawn to the horror of this whole scene.

I wish I could talk about my feelings with someone, but the others in this house only wish to escape when they come here after working at the relief effort all day. We play cards, gossip, read, listen to music, and then someone will mention the latest news or the latest rumor, and we are off and running about our daily lives, but we are afraid to look into each other's eyes and say, out loud, "How do you *feel* about this?" Maybe we are afraid of starting to unwind a very large, very tightly wrapped roll of gauze.

✦ ✦ ✦

My students began to sprinkle their conversations with "secession." On the radio, hints about "one Nigeria" cropped up on the news read from Lagos, while diatribes against "the Hausas" or "the Northerners" was a daily occurrence when I picked up the news from Enugu or Port Harcourt. Every week, there was some report of an incident to do with the isolation the East was suffering. It was rumored one day that the Rivers people were going to rise up against the Ibos in support of the Federal government; there was a rumor another day that the Rivers people were going to be the first defenders of the Eastern Region, seeing as they were living nearest the ocean, and would protect the Ibos. My students believed it all, swaying from one rumor to the next.

✦ ✦ ✦

Even though I can still only say about 10 words in Yoruba, whenever I use them the men I supervise slap my hands and slap someone else's hands in delight.

In Biafra, the Yorubas were one of the enemies. I think of that whenever one of the men puts his arm around me.

✦ ✦ ✦

"This rain!" Charlie cries as he pushes the patio doors shut to keep us from being flooded.

I get up from the couch to help him. "God, I love the rains here!" I say, even as I get sprayed with the water splashing onto the cement patio.

It does not drizzle. It pours. It crashes down, inches of water in hours, day after day. If you get caught in it, you are drenched. Umbrellas are mostly useless, as the rain twists and swirls, playing a game with you, getting you wet all over.

Yet, I am fascinated with the force and the suddenness of these African rains. In fact, in our household, only Monty complains.

✛   ✛   ✛

The Harmattan came as a surprise, even though I had been warned. I actually got chilled! I loved the foggy mornings and the dry days that lacked the intense heat, sun, and humidity of the rest of the time. The students wore blue cardigan sweaters over their white uniforms. They asked me, constantly, how I felt. Was I cold? Did I find this weather different from home? Did I like the rain? Did I think the Eastern Region would secede? Did I like coconut?

✛   ✛   ✛

I am desperate to get to the field. Bulle promises me that he will get me on a medical/food team as quickly as possible, but nothing has come of it yet. They are waiting to get into the Port Harcourt area, so I may get back to my old stomping grounds.

I dream about going back, but in the dream I cannot talk, and the people, whose faces I recognize, are looking just to my left and won't or can't look at me. I reach out for them, but, in that eerie way dreams have, my arms won't reach them, although we are standing very close. I reach and reach, and mutter and mutter, and suddenly I am awake, moaning, my mouth held tightly closed, my arms flailing in the air. My mouth opens suddenly and I cry out, "Aaahhh!"

I dream it again and again and again. And each time, I end it by crying out, pulling my mouth open to its fullest, "Aaahhh!"

I ride to work some mornings with my airport supervisor, a fat Swiss. I am beginning to think "fat Swiss" is redundant. He sits in his office at the other end of the airport and fills out forms, smokes, and tries to get his Nigerian secretary into bed. She is resisting him. I am cheering her on. He attempts to rub her leg and even her breasts when we three ride back into the city, crowded together in the front of his little Peugeot lorry. I ride a taxi back and forth to work more and more.

✛   ✛   ✛

A MiG is practicing on the far runway. We assume the pilot is Nigerian, or perhaps Egyptian or Russian since they are providing pilots and pilot training. He comes in as if to land, skims the ground, and flies up again. Then he circles, and repeats the maneuver. Charlie tells a story: An Egyptian pilot flies close to the ground, upside down. A Nigerian pilot witnesses it, and takes up his own plane to do the same thing. Without practicing anything, he turns the plane upside down, begins his descent, and simply smashes into the ground. End of story. If it's even true. We hear so many things and there's that old expatriate habit of rushing these kinds of stories around, not caring if they're true or not.

These planes are bombing the markets where the Biafrans have gathered, and the hospitals where the wounded are lying under the protection of giant red crosses on the roofs.

The next time this plane comes by I want to stand in the way and throw rocks. Hungary 1956.

I fantasize that I am captured by the Biafrans, that one of them is a former student, that I am set free and am allowed to work in a clinic on that side of the war. Then I come back to reality and look at the foodstuffs piled around me in the shed at the airport at Lagos.

✛   ✛   ✛

Only last year—it seems so much longer ago than that—we sailed into this same Lagos on the ship that evacuated us from Biafra. NBC was there. We could hear Linda being interviewed. I was jealous.

"What's your name?" asked the man with the microphone. She told him.

"Where are you from?" he asked.

"Biafra," she said. She was supposed to say "Oklahoma."

I looked around to see if any Nigerians overheard her. "Enemy territory," I said in a low voice to someone.

✛   ✛   ✛

I look around now. I'm not sure whose territory I think it is.

I mention to one of the top brass of the Red Cross here that I am part Swiss. His attitude towards me changes immediately. It even turns out that my ancestors came from the same canton he is from. Now, instead of being one more ignorant American who speaks only a smattering of German and French, I am the descendant of noble people. I wish I had shut up.

I wear a Red Cross on my shirt. "The easier to aim at you," says Charlie. He has been to the front already.

I don't know how much longer I can sit at the airport with little to do all day except help unload the wounded and load our supplies. Most of the time we are waiting, waiting, waiting. I sit and bullshit with the men who load the planes.

And so much of what we are given to ship out is useless: Tin cans of food that Nigerian villagers aren't used to, like the flavored puddings sent out to Lagos by well-meaning souls in England.

We save such items until there is nothing else possible to go out and then we load case after case on the planes and hope someone can make use of them, somewhere.

One of the relief workers complained that it is bad enough we have to send out the puddings, but there are no can openers anywhere to open the cans. Openers have been requested, but none has arrived so far.

It's mad.

✢   ✢   ✢

I don't have those dreams anymore, the ones I had in Malawi. I had the same one at least once a week there: In the dream, I arrived back in Biafra and found that everything was all right, after all. I grabbed my students and friends and danced with them, laughing and crying, so happy that everything was really OK. Then, suddenly, in the middle of our dancing arm-in-arm, I would wake up, and the truth would come to me, all in a rush, and I would shudder and gasp. I dared God to give me that dream once again. And, every few days, I received it, and cursed God all the more.

✢   ✢   ✢

Bucks and I are standing on the tarmac, waiting for his DC-4 to be loaded when he turns to me and says, with a sigh, "We're either feedin' 'em or killin' 'em!" He flicks his cigarette away from the plane.

"Oh?" I say, not sure if that is what he means.

"Yeah," he answers, seeming to expect the kind of response he gets. "Yeah, we're either carryin' this stuff—" He points to the pallets. "Or we got guns in here to take to the front. Feedin' or killin'." He spits, then reaches for another Camel.

The red cross on the white circle on the tail is still wet. It gets repainted every time we use the plane for food. When the tail is blank, we know what is going east.

✛ ✛ ✛

"Al haji! Al haji!" the men and women cry. The pilgrims arriving home from Mecca have broad smiles. The government uses half of our storage shed as the welcoming center for the pilgrims. We look over the partition from our side and join in the waving. One of the men who works with me intends to go to Mecca as soon as he can save the money. His eyes gleam with pride whenever another planeload arrives. *"Al haji!"* he cries to the men decked out in their finest. *"Al haji!"* I am caught up in the excitement, and, after some initial concern that I'm not supposed to do this since I am not a Muslim, I too wave and cry out, *"Al haji! Al haji!"*

✛ ✛ ✛

The radio talked of massacres, of genocide, of Northern Nigerians, Hausas mostly, killing Ibos in Kano and Kaduna and Zaria. Wiping out a merchant class with machetes and guns. The Eastern government and press called it a "pogrom."

Our school secretary stood in my living room, wildly gesturing. "Those Muslims! They hate us Ibos! They kill us!" He snapped his fingers, wiped his forehead with his white handkerchief, and exhaled an "aaahhh."

Martin, a Peace Corps Volunteer who lived 20 miles east of my school, sat in my house with a student of his. They had returned from a long two days in Port Harcourt where they had gone to help take care of the survivors flown south from the Northern region.

"They got off the planes from the North—" Martin began and the student, Isaac, interrupted. "Some with no arms," Isaac said. "Some with one leg."

I grimaced. "One man had hidden in the house of a friend, also an Ibo," Martin said. "But a neighbor told somebody and a mob came and got him."

"Was he on the plane, too?" I asked.

"Oh, no, he was killed in Kano," Martin said. "I just heard about it from a friend of his."

Before he left with Isaac, Martin told of seeing a Northerner killed by a mob in the streets of Port Harcourt, in retaliation for the killings in the North. Isaac whistled through his teeth when Martin finished.

"Terrible," he said. "Terrible."

Even we expatriates, from that day on, felt isolated, alone, already seceded.

✛　✛　✛

"*Al haji!*" continues to be shouted in the shed and outside where still more well-wishers are standing. I go back to work, counting boxes of food.

✛　✛　✛

My supervisor waves the woman away from the lorry window. "Go!" he cries.

"Wait!" I say in an unusually harsh voice with him. "Damnit, she only wants to ask you something!"

He starts the motor, pretending he doesn't hear me.

The woman is showing him samples of foodstuffs—vegetables, eggs, dried fish. "I give you good price. Red Cross price. You buy plenty, no?"

"Go!" he cries. I put my hand on his arm.

"Tell her to take them upstairs. Bulle's in charge of that."

He starts to back up, almost knocking the lorry's front fender against the woman. She cries out.

"Stop!" I shout at him. He finally looks up. He stops. "Madam," I say across him through his window. "Take-m up that place. Doc-tor Bull-lee," I say slowly, enunciating every syllable. "Doc-tor Bull-lee, he go look-am."

She smiles, showing missing teeth, and runs that way.

"Damn!" I say. We drive on.

✦ ✦ ✦

The story is not one I've heard before, but it comes from a reliable source, a Red Cross woman from Paris who has just been to the front. She is sitting in our living room, and we gather about her, eagerly awaiting news from someone who was in Enugu this morning, and very near the front lines only yesterday afternoon. "It is amazing," she says, pausing to inhale her little Gaullois. "The Nigerian soldiers are caring for so many orphans. And they are feeding the old people from their own food. We must get in some of those areas and bring more food quickly. They cannot do it adequately this way."

I frown. This does not jibe with the stories of the atrocities, the "genocide," the soldiers who shoot deliberately at civilians, who kill Ibos as if they were rabbits at the height of the season.

✦ ✦ ✦

We are watching the men and women dance the High Life through the smoke and our own fog caused by having drunk a little too much beer. The man comes up, and, without asking, pulls a chair to the front of our table, right in my line of vision, and helps himself down into it. He places his crutches against the side of the table. The left pant leg is folded neatly over and over again until it reaches the rest of his leg, somewhere near his groin. If he still has a groin.

Monty and I are at the club to enjoy ourselves, drinking and maybe dancing. This man does not fit into our Saturday-night plans. He belongs to the daytime world, Monday to Saturday, maybe at the airport, stumbling out of a military plane fresh from the war zone, or hobbling along the Marina, glowering at the shoppers who do not see him.

Why does he choose this place to sit down? There are other tables. He reaches for my cigarettes and does not ask me for approval.

Why is he here? He certainly isn't going to dance.

The waitress brings him a beer, and I half-expect him to point to us to pay for it, but he reaches into a shirt pocket and takes out a pound note. He says nothing to us. He drinks quietly and quickly in small sips, then takes a puff now and then from the cigarette and knocks the ash off onto the floor. I find myself staring at his profile.

Monty and I have become silent. We do not look at one another. I am almost angry. He does not belong here, I say to myself once again. This was our chance to get away, like most of the rest of Lagos is doing, and forget the war, although most of the rest of Lagos seems to do that pretty well every day. It seems more my war than it is theirs.

+ + +

Many Saturday nights we went to the Lido in Port Harcourt. The music was loud, the large bottles of Star beer and Guinness stout kept arriving at our table, paid for by one of us or all of us.

The High Life! We would go on to the dance floor, yelling loudly as we made our way there when we heard a particular tune we loved, and dance and dance and dance. At one point in the music, the drums would take over and we would be mesmerized, dancing with our eyes half open, dancing with our eyes half closed, moving our hips in staccato beats, causing an occasional Nigerian to shout and point to our buttocks with delight.

Moving back and forth, hands in the air, index fingers pointed upwards, slowly twirling them about, as we advanced towards our partners, getting very close, then backing away several steps, always gyrating our hips, moving our butts, with only a little shoulder movement, turning to the side, keeping one hand, finger extended, in the air, while we lay the other palm, flat against our stomach, then facing our partners again, then to the other side, then back again, then, once in a while, twirl in a circle, both hands again in the air, higher and higher ... smiling, smiling, smiling.

Life was good. Life was wonderful. It could not possibly be better.

+ + +

I have an eerie sensation that this man is a figment of our imagination, that he is here, like some kind of Dickens ghost, to remind us that we are not here to have fun, but to proceed with the war. I want to reach over and touch him, or see my fingers go through him to prove that he is not here. The colored lights move across the dance floor and suddenly, briefly, I get a good look at his face. He is young. Of course. I motion for Monty to lean towards me and I whisper, "Shall we go?" and he says nothing, but nods his head.

Outside, we walk until we find a taxi and make our way home. We don't speak in the cab, or in the house, not even to say goodnight.

I want to go to bed, and get a good night's sleep, free of any dreams that might intrude to remind me even while asleep of what is going on in this part of the world and what is going on in my mind when I'm awake.

I want tears, but I can't bring them forth. I want tears for the man on the stretcher, for the buddy with one arm, for the nightclub man who forced his one-legged presence on us. Tears for me, damnit.

OCTOBER 1968 – LAGOS

I am returning to Port Harcourt. Whenever I think about it, I pause and breathe deeply, and bite the inside of my bottom lip.

I am traveling with two Nigerian pre-med students from the University of Ibadan, Benjamin and Gabriel. Both are in their second year of school and are being sent out by the Nigerian Red Cross to work with a medical team. The three of us are eager to be out of Lagos and into the thick of it.

I have been warned: Don't expect it to be like you left it. Don't think you'll find much of anything there. Kingsway is burned down, you know, it's only a shell. I know that. I remember reading about that. The Nigerians blamed the Biafrans; the Biafrans blamed the Nigerians. Such a fuss over one department store.

✛ ✛ ✛

Saturday mornings, I went up the two flights of escalators to drink Dutch-made chocolate milk and eat warm, slightly greasy pastry in Kingsway's top-floor canteen.

We Volunteers played a game: We looked at prices neatly printed on white gummed labels on the bottoms of thorn carvings and statues made of wood and horn, and righteously clucked our tongues at how much we had saved by bargaining for them only blocks away in the main market.

One fine Saturday morning, the woman behind the grocery counter cut a large slice of Gouda and slipped me a note under it, inviting me to her house after work. "Rose of Kingsway" she called herself in the note, and she smiled her big, fat face at me and shook her head so her wig moved slightly and her gold earrings reflected the fluorescent ceiling lights.

She gave me a conspiratorial wink. Her smile was expectant, her lips moist. "I see you here every Saturday," she said in a stage whisper. "Come my house. I be fine woman-o."

I smiled and fled with my Gouda.

✠   ✠   ✠

We, and the world, receive word that four Red Cross workers have been killed by Nigerians in the "liberation" of Okigwi. I was in Okigwi once; beautiful little town with a pottery shop. Somewhere in the South Atlantic there is a ship carrying a cream-and-sugar set of Okigwi pottery to my parents.

Somebody made a mistake. They were not to have been killed. I know somebody made a mistake. And, to think that I had some confidence in the wearing of this red badge on my pocket. Four of 'em. And they got as much—no, more—coverage in the world press, no doubt, as all the black Nigerians and black Biafrans who died the same day. Our white skin is a kind of status, a kind of protection. We feel it envelop us; it is our Saran Wrap. And yet, we too die. The only difference is the world learns our names.

✠   ✠   ✠

I bid farewell to the orange-coveralled work crew I supervised at the airport, to the fat Swiss man who sits smoking cigars and filling out forms, and to his secretary who continues to look uncomfortable. Come to think of it, her name is Rose, too, but she is alive, and the Rose of Kingsway is probably dead, or else she is traveling with the troops of one side or another. I imagine she is thinner.

We board a very familiar DC-4, one of those we have loaded so many times. The students are surprised there are no seats.

Benjamin, the older one, whistles through his teeth, and stops momentarily and looks at me as if we have made a mistake. Gabriel laughs to himself. I explain that the seats have been removed to make room for cargo. Benjamin takes out a white handkerchief, shakes it and places it on the floor, up against a wall. He sits down with a frown, and dusts off his hands.

Gabriel does the same. I sit down beside them without protection. We feel the plane begin to taxi to the runway. We have never flown this way before, and it is fun, yet it is so frightening, especially when I think of all the times the stewardesses have come by to make sure all of us have our seat belts fastened. Now, we not only have no belts, we have no seats, and the rough interior of the plane contains so many pointed, metal places where we could slam ourselves silly if the plane hit any turbulence. Or we could be thrown against the cargo—boxes and barrels filled with mysterious things. Nevertheless, I laugh to myself and shrug my shoulders. We all move so we can see out the windows and watch Lagos grow smaller and smaller and disappear under its own pollution. For most of the trip, we fly over palm trees so thick you can't see the ground, or along beautiful beaches where you rarely see anyone.

✛ ✛ ✛

Dr. Bulle has given me instructions: Go to Calabar, then fly across the river to Uyo, and get from there to Port Harcourt by land, using a vehicle belonging to the Red Cross in the Uyo area. The Port Harcourt people don't know exactly when we're coming; in fact, they probably don't expect us for a couple of weeks.

I'm not sure exactly what my job will be. I am so eager to be there, back in the area where I once lived, that I am willing to do anything. I think of my teaching experiences, my students, my friends, my school, even my house, and the thoughts of reunion with all those people and with all those places come over me, until I am jolted with the reality that so many of those people must surely already be dead.

✛ ✛ ✛

I wrote an essay for my fifth formers that drew their applause. It was written as if the author were one of them and it talked about living in two worlds, the traditional one and the modern one, and how it was so challenging for them.

I had put a lot of emotion into the writing of it, having observed the difficulties the students were having, and they rewarded me with absolute cheers.

This was one of those times that I reached them so fully, so well, helping to make up for the other times that I failed completely to understand something that seemed so obvious or so important to them. Then, out of frustration, I might simply bury myself in Faulkner or The New York Times *and pretend I was living in Manhattan.*

✦ ✦ ✦

We go up, one by one, to see the cockpit, and watch all the controls with their little indicators jerking back and forth. I have never been in a cockpit and I wonder why they don't keep their eyes more on the dials. Can everything be working all right?

✦ ✦ ✦

Fortunately, there is no turbulence, although it rains most of the trip. We huddle together so we can hear one another over the roar of the engines.

It begins to rain very hard. Suddenly, the plane starts to circle. On the ground below is what we think is Calabar. I begin to worry: Why aren't we landing? There can't be any other planes around, except occasional military ones. I can see the airport out of my window. The rain and wind are beginning to wear on the three of us, and the motion of continually circling is making me feel slightly ill.

The plane doesn't sound right. I wonder if we are going to crash. We are tilted at a crazy angle, as we circle and circle. The engines sound terrible. The circles seem to be getting smaller, the plane seems to be circling more, pushing us against one another. I decide to ask the pilots what's wrong, but when I approach them, each glances my way, a deep frown on his face, and they turn back to the front, silently, ignoring my shouted questions. Now I am truly worried, but I don't want the students to know.

"What's going on?" asks Benjamin. Gabriel looks up.

I fake a smile, and then say, "They didn't answer. I don't know. Probably waiting for some general's plane to land."

All at once, we go into a straight run again, and I am knocked down, right into the students, and my cigarette goes flying. I retrieve it quickly, crawling across the rough flooring, afraid it will start a fire. The floor is covered with thick grease and oil stains. I crawl to the windows to join Gabriel and Benjamin. We discover we are leaving Calabar, but we can't agree on what direction we are heading.

✛   ✛   ✛

When the plane begins to descend, we crawl to the windows once again. I stare out, my face pressed to the glass, and all at once Benjamin says, "It must be Port Harcourt!"

"Port Harcourt!" I am so excited. I can't verify whether it is or not; I feel I should be able to recognize the city, but I am confused by the direction we are flying in, and the rain makes everything into a look-alike gray mass.

Suddenly, we are landing. We sit back and brace ourselves. As soon as we have come to a halt, and the noise stops, the pilots get out of their seats. Smitty comes back to us. "Port Harcourt, boys!"

"So it *is* P.H.!" I say. "What happened back there?"

"Couldn't land! Too much wind and rain. We thought we could wait it out, but that was some fuckin' storm. What a bitch! Had to come over here." He smiles. One of his teeth has a gold cap. "We'll leave as soon as we can and go back."

Suddenly it dawns on me. "We can get off here! We're supposed to end up in P.H., anyway."

Smitty shakes his head. "Nope, no can do. Military orders. From the man in charge of this whole area of the war himself, Col. Adekunle." Smitty makes a mock salute. "Can't let anybody off without prior *pur-mish-un*. If we do, ol' 'Black Scorpion' Adekunle'll have our ass. Yours too." He quickly looks at the door. He lowers his voice. "That Adekunle. Jesus, that guy's crazy!"

It seems so bureaucratic, so silly. Here we are in Port Harcourt, our final destination, and we can't get off the plane. But the mention of Adekunle's name cools any desire to disobey and just leap out and make our way to the Red Cross people here. Gossip has it that even General Gowon who is supposed to be in charge of the whole *country* is worried about Adekunle. The Black Scorpion is a little like Caesar. Lagos worries: Will the Niger become the Rubicon? When he—or if he—mops up this area, as he says so often that he's going to do in a very short time, he may fly back to Lagos and take over the country by popular support. And by the use of a couple of well-placed guns, possibly aimed at the head of state.

I have never been to this airport before. I have been past the cement bunker at the entrance; it was hurriedly constructed shortly before secession. It reminded me instantly of the films where the Nazis are holed up in one and the brave Americans creep up and toss grenades inside. I wonder if the bunker is still there—or if some brave Nigerian crept up and threw a grenade in on the Biafran defenders.

I see the blatant signs highlighting Gowon and the words "One Nigeria" everywhere, and amuse myself by thinking how shocking it would have been to have had them here when this was Biafran soil.

We see the burned-out plane at the side of the runway, although all of us are careful not to point to it. "That's one of these guys' planes," I say. Benjamin nods.

"What happened to it, do you know?" he asks.

"Yep. Smitty told me. One of our forklift trucks at the airport, that same one that loaded these pallets today, bumped into the door. Like this one right here. I was there, on the ground. I still remember Smitty screaming at the guy who did it, and the door never really shut right after that."

"Look!" says Gabriel. "There's the same door. Right there, in the grass."

"Wait, let him finish," says Benjamin.

"A couple weeks later," I say, "there were about fifty soldiers on board, all decked out in heavy gear, and the door flew open right as they were coming in to land. They all ran away from the open door, and the plane went out of control."

"All killed?"

"Uh-huh. One of the soldiers managed to survive for a couple of days. That's how they found out what happened. Poof!" I say, gesturing towards the sky. "All of 'em. Gone. Just like that."

We are silent. Then I add, "They say the mortars on board were exploding all night long. That's why so little of the plane is still left, I guess."

What does remain sits there, its edges blackened like a poorly done piece of toast, and the gray and blue of the rest of the plane is burnt here and there, or miraculously intact here and there. It seems to mock us and our own DC-4. I am thinking of getting out to walk around when Smitty and the other pilot reappear. The storm has left Calabar and gone out to sea, and we're leaving immediately.

We speak briefly at the open door to the Nigerians who are wandering about on the tarmac below. One speaks Yoruba with Benjamin and Gabriel. "Cigarette?" another calls up to me, and I smile and shake my head. I am glad I left the pack on the floor by my trunk, or else I would be obligated to share one with him, and then one each with his suddenly appearing friends, and I am not sure just how long my few packs will last. I don't expect to find many cigarettes once we've settled in.

✛ ✛ ✛

I boarded the ki-ki bus at the edge of the school compound, after shouting "Port Harcourt!" at the driver and at his assistant who was hanging out the back of the bus, signaling to the driver to stop and go by pounding hard on the metal roof.

The buses were the size of VW vans, with wooden benches along the sides. In the middle, the space filled with small children, large bundles taken from the heads of the women, small suitcases, sometimes live chickens.

"Hello, white man!" someone always said with delight. I would nod my head, accept his offered hand, and shake it. If I snapped his finger in return for his snapping mine, the attention of the passengers increased. If I argued with the assistant over the price of the bus and offered the same fare the others were offering, I was asked, "Are you really a white man?"

I was never sure at the onset of shaking hands if I were going to be able, that time, to make the fingers snap they way they showed us in Peace Corps training. Pushing your middle fingers very hard against one another's, then pulling back, fast and hard. If successful, one could hear the results. If not, an impotent quiet, with a disappointed look on my face—and my hand, dangling.

Flurries of Igbo and Pidgin English surrounded me. Conversations on other topics ceased in order to discuss this incredible sight: a white man paying the same price as a Nigerian.

How could that be?! Laughter broke out, men snapped their fingers in enthusiastic handshakes and old women, seemingly always too loud and too shrill, let loose with commentary that had the whole bus laughing, including me who hardly understood anything at all they were saying.

"White man!" an old woman would cry out, her hands held against her head as if she were in shock. "You be too much! Too much!"

✛   ✛   ✛

Tall palm trees stand like guards along the sides of the runway. I feel comfort in them. I had missed them in Lagos although along the Marina there are many, but there they seem to belong to the churches, the hotels, the government homes and the clubs that line that boulevard. Here, they are no one's and I like that. I take comfort in palm trees, I think again, and I want to share that with the students, but I realize they will probably not understand what I am talking about. Each was raised in a village, so being close to palm trees is perhaps too ordinary. It's like me with oaks and maples. (No, that's not right. After years of being away from oaks and maples, I miss them terribly.)

The cargo door is shut and locked by Smitty, and I am suddenly sorry I told the story of the other plane's demise to Gabriel and Benjamin. They each ask me if I think the door is securely fastened, and I assure them it is, although I really have no idea, but we decide to move to the opposite side of the plane, and down a little ways, just to feel safer. I really don't want to be pulled out an open door, to float downward to my palm trees far below, an ocean away from oaks and maples.

✛   ✛   ✛

I was glad I was not driving. The Port Harcourt traffic was once again at a standstill, each lorry, each van, each car trying hard to take the lead whenever the vehicles ahead moved up a few inches. Everyone was shouting. Van assistants were banging on the tops of their vans, laughing, shouting, cursing, adding to the din.

Roads that were supposed to be two lanes wide were six or seven. Pedestrians actually attempted to cross the road, causing everyone to yell at them. "Silly woman! Is this a motor park?"

shouted one, gesturing broadly to indicate the dozens of cars that were poised to run her down, should she somehow not see them there.

And the dust. Wind blew and it was stirred up. The traffic churned it up into the air. It got into one's eyes, one's nose.

Soon, the traffic moved enough to get turned onto a side street and the ki-ki bus moved quickly, taking advantage of the sudden freedom. We arrived at the motor park and the impatient passengers jumped from the van and scattered on their errands, while those with boxes tied to the top waited for it to reach its destination inside the walls.

I alighted as soon as I could, dusted off my clothes, waved to the assistant, nodded to two old women who had never stopped talking about me, and hurried on my way.

✛　✛　✛

Calabar this time is clear, and we land, bumping along the runway, knocking against one another, laughing with relief. We shake hands, rapidly and enthusiastically. For once, I make the requisite loud snap and we laugh in delight.

We are searched by friendly soldiers who are curious about us and our belongings; they don't seem to be really searching for anything. We are standing below the cargo door when our trunks are lowered; we try to help but the Nigerians doing the unloading wave us away.

"Petrol! Move aside! Move aside!" one of them suddenly shouts, and we look up to see 50-gallon red drums about to descend through the air. We move back quickly, putting dozens of yards between us and the plane, and an incredible routine begins: The drums are dropped onto a mammoth tire. They bounce into the air, then hit the runway and roll for several yards, making smaller and smaller bounces, until the men catch them and roll them to the side of the runway. They seem to find this a game, but the three of us are horrified. If one explodes, the whole airplane would go. I didn't even know we were carrying petrol. And there I sat on the floor of the plane, smoking to calm my nerves. God!

✛　✛　✛

As soon as I was settled in at my school, I taped a large map of Nigeria to the wall. Almost every day, I would look at it, planning trips to Calabar or Kano or the Jos Plateau. I smiled at the occasional plane that flew overhead, anticipating a vacation to somewhere else in Nigeria, this new world of mine. The luxury of a plane ride, looking out the window at the peaceful landscape, was the daydream I had when students quietly worked on a writing assignment in class or I raised my head from grading papers at my dining table and saw the vast country laid out before me, beckoning me from across the room.

✛　✛　✛

I arrange with one of the UNICEF workers, an American named Roger, to fly us to Uyo with our trunks. I'll try to borrow a Land Rover to get us to Port Harcourt from there. In the belly of the large chopper I rest my arm on my own trunk, and look at the Cross River below. I wonder if they'll ever be able to build a bridge from the Calabar side to the Uyo side. There is no sign of life, no boats, even small ones, and I conclude that the land is not really land, but tree trunks, one mangrove tree butted up against another, and repeated millions of times, islands of trees separated by the river and its tributaries, in a mind-boggling display of wet, green life. I think of snakes.

✛　✛　✛

I stepped over a pencil on the living room floor. Then I did a double take. Pencils did not move and have little tongues darting in and out. I wheeled around and confronted a snake the size of a pencil. I screamed.

Godfrey came running in from the kitchen. He spied the snake, cried out, letting out a series of short, panicky sounds, then ran out of the house. In an instant, he returned with a machete and the snake was cut into dozens of wriggling pieces. Godfrey swept up the remains and carried it outside.

He and I agreed totally about snakes: All of them are poisonous and all of them should be killed. No exceptions.

✛　✛　✛

I recall the stories about Adekunle and his treatment of his own men. He is said to have been driving down the road one day after he had captured Port Harcourt from the Biafrans when he spotted a man wearing tennis shoes with his army uniform. Not bothering to ask anything, he had his driver stop, then he got out and shot the tennis-shoed soldier through the head. Perhaps the man had sold his regulation Nigerian-army-issued shoes. Maybe they had been stolen by another soldier. Maybe he never was issued any in the first place. I laughed it off when I first heard it. Biafran propaganda. Nigerian propaganda, for different purposes. Now, flying over land controlled by Adekunle, I choose to believe it.

✥   ✥   ✥

At Uyo, not one of the Red Cross people has ever heard of our scheme for getting the three of us to P.H. One of the men, upon hearing we had actually been at the Port Harcourt airport earlier in the day, tells me that we should have insisted on getting off, that Adekunle, unless he was actually at the airport, would never had known. "Go back to Calabar and get on the next flight to Port Harcourt," he says. "We can't spare any transport here, anyway. I don't know what the hell Bulle is talking about."

✥   ✥   ✥

I ride with a Save the Children person to a center in Uyo where children are being fed. We have two hours before we catch the helicopter back to Calabar. The man in charge of the center, a young Nigerian, almost does not shake my hand. His questions are curt, his stare at me is condescending. He walks through the compound, his movements scattering the children. Some of the girls are in dresses, the buttons missing, the garments open all the way. Some are naked. It is a typical village scene, only there are almost no adults as there would be in a village. Some of the children are sitting on the ground, staring listlessly across the dirt yard.

He stops in the middle and waves his arms. "Are you shocked?" His lips seem to curl and he pulls his head back in a defiance I have rarely seen in a Nigerian.

"No," I reply, honestly.

He says nothing, but raises his eyebrows. He seems almost to believe me.

"I've lived in Nigeria before. Most of these children don't look any worse than the average village child."

He relaxes. "We get so many foreigners here, so many," he says, shaking his head. "They cannot understand why we don't have clothing on all the children, why they don't have shoes, why their bellies are so big. 'But they seem so well fed to me,' some woman said here one day. British!" He says it with contempt, spitting out "British."

I kneel down and smile at one of the children. I gently squeeze her chin, and wink at her, something that has always made Nigerian children burst into gales of laughter and rapid chatter. She gives me a faint smile, and there is a tired look in her eyes. "*Beke*," she whispers, and I am reminded that my racial classification is uppermost in her mind. She raises a very thin arm and pats the side of my face, and then drops her arm and stands there, looking at me. There is no movement, even her eyes do not dart back and forth excitedly. Instead, they focus on my face somewhere, and are held in place. I can't give up. I chuck her under her chin once again, and she frowns, and pulls her face to the side. I have never seen a child react like this.

Now, I am shocked.

✛   ✛   ✛

Every time I rode my bicycle into the village, dozens of small children ran to the edge of the roadway and cried out, "Onye ocha! Onye ocha!" I waved, smiled and shouted, "Hello!" which sent them into frenzies of delight. I could not begin to imagine how strange I must look to them. The only white people they would ever see were those who went roaring by inside automobiles. I, on the other hand, was on foot or on a bicycle. They could get up close. Whenever I made a face at them, they froze for a second, then screamed with delight and ran to their mothers, yelling excitedly all the way. The only words I understood were "onye ocha."

I began to tire of it. It would never stop. As children became able to walk and to run, they would join the groups. I could have gone through this village for a decade and the flow of screaming children would never end.

I asked one of the teachers, "If I'm 'onye ocha,' what are you?" and he said, "Onye ogi." I bided my time. Soon, I was on my bicycle again, heading into the village. The children, as usual, came running, crying out, waving, yelling the familiar words. Instead of waving back or smiling, I slowed down, and shouted, "Onye ogi!"

There was stunned silence. Then, the group burst into laughter. They screamed once more with delight and rushed to their mothers to tell them. I now understood two sets of words in their conversation. The mothers, in turn, screamed with delight and called out to me, waving and laughing. I smiled triumphantly and rode on.

The next time I went through the village, nothing had changed. The children ran at me, crying out, waving, laughing. My reply of "Onye ogi!" sent them into familiar gales of laughter. I was doomed to engage in this harmless silliness for the rest of my stay.

✦   ✦   ✦

After waiting hours at the Calabar airport, watching the choppers come and go and come and go, we are able to get on a small Nigerian military aircraft that has had most of its seats taken out. Our trunks go inside with us and become places for six people to sit. I am idly looking out the window as we near Port Harcourt when I suddenly realize I am staring at the refinery only a couple of miles from my old school. But, instead of large white tanks decorated in oil-company names and filled with petrol and oil, there are black splotches on the ground, as if someone had lifted the tanks away and spilled a black powdery ink so that it hit in the center and blew out in all directions. The tanks that do remain seem lonely indeed.

"Look!" I grab Benjamin's arm. "See that? That's the school where I used to teach!" The roof of the main building is caved in on one side. The rest of the campus seems all right in a quick glance.

"Was it bombed?" Benjamin asks.

"Must have been. Why else would there be such a mess like that? There's my house! The yellow one. Over there." I can see no one on the campus nor any vehicles there or on the roads in view. I keep the school in sight for all the seconds I can, and absent-mindedly wave good-bye to it as it disappears just as we come in for our landing at the airport.

The plane has been crowded with civilians; most of them, we guess quietly to one another, are relatives of army officers, or high-ranking civilians in the government.

One man who is sitting on a lone propane tank is persuaded by several of us not to light his cigarette. He is reluctant, almost defiant, then he puts the pack back into his pocket.

✦ ✦ ✦

Whenever I visited a student in his village, I was given a large bottle of Star beer to drink. A glass was found for me, hurriedly washed and dried, amid much loud conversation. The bottle and glass were set upon a table placed in front of me. Soon, two or three individual cigarettes were placed on the table, too. I was invited to smoke and drink. Sometimes, my offer of a cigarette or some of the beer to the father was accepted; other times, it was gratefully refused. I could not drink a whole big bottle of Star beer without feeling somewhat high. I began to wonder if I would remember anything about my years in Nigeria, or would they all be lost in some semi-alcoholic haze?

✦ ✦ ✦

It is dark by the time we get inside the small terminal. Suddenly, I don't know what to do. All our energies have been devoted to getting here, and now that we're here, reason and any organizational ability I have been displaying leave me. Benjamin seems to understand and says to us, "Wait. I'll see what we can do."

He goes over to a tall Indian or Pakistani and engages him in conversation. Gabriel and I sit down in two of the few chairs available. Benjamin returns and says, "We're in luck. That man I spoke to is working with the military command. And," he adds, smiling, "that's the same place the Red Cross is staying. He's got room in his car for only one of us. I'll bring back one of the Red Cross people to collect you and the trunks."

✦ ✦ ✦

He seems to be gone forever. I try to doze, then I try to stay awake, and the mosquitoes begin to make their awful dive-bomber noises inside my outer ears. All at once, Benjamin enters with a blond guy. "This is Ralph," Benjamin says.

We jump up. I hold out my hand. "Hi, I'm—"

"Get in the Land Rover outside!" Ralph almost hisses. "Hurry!"

We move quickly, and the four of us load our trunks in the back, then jump inside. "What's wrong?" I ask when we are all inside.

"Wrong! God in heaven! You're not supposed to be here. Adekunle'll go mad if he finds out. Dr. Martin is almost hysterical. I can't believe Bulle pulled this!"

"But I thought—"

"It's not your fault. I know that, it's just that when Benjamin showed up and announced that you three had arrived, the shit hit the fan, believe me."

I get a queasy feeling in my stomach. "What about Adekunle?"

"He won't know, thank God, and he's not going to, even after we get you out of here and back to Lagos tomorrow."

"Tomorrow!"

"Tomorrow. Dr. Martin said he'll get you on the Cessna that comes through here every day. It's usually pretty empty going back to Lagos."

Gabriel begins to speak. "But Dr. Bulle said everything would be all right."

"Well, that's his opinion. It's not all right, believe me. Adekunle runs this place like it's a concentration camp. He even shoots his own soldiers. Nobody goes in or out without his permission, and when—if—he finds out you're here, I don't know what he'll do to all of us. That's what worries Dr. Martin. Did you hear what Adekunle did to our Land Rovers when we first arrived?"

"No."

"We'd been here, and I'm not exaggerating, not more than five minutes from our drive over from Uyo, and we had just gone inside the mess hall to eat when some of Adekunle's soldiers came along and painted out the words "The International Committee of" from the sides of all our vehicles. He only left "The Red Cross."

"But why?"

"He despises the ICRC. We don't know why, exactly. And everyone is afraid to ask him for fear he'll get it in his head to do something else to us, like forbid us from leaving P.H. to start up some clinics. The only reason we're here is because Gowon said he had to take us."

"So he does obey Gowon now and then." I smile.

"You bet he does. For now, at least." He waves a bug away from his face. "We're busy tiptoeing around Adekunle's egomania, and it's constant, hard work to keep up a job like that. But if we don't, we could be kicked out."

"Where will we stay tonight?"

"We'll hide you in our quarters. We're right beside the mess hall. Then we'll get you out to the Red Cross Cessna early tomorrow morning."

I stop listening to the conversation that continues between Ralph and Benjamin and stare out a window to see what I can of Port Harcourt. I know this street. It leads from Aba to downtown P.H., and I traveled it at least weekly for a year. But I can hardly recognize it. I can't quite believe it, but there is not one little fire, not one light, not one vehicle, not one *anything*. Just us, moving along at a cautious speed, past miles of abandoned buildings. A city that was almost 200,000 now turned into a ghost town.

"Where is everybody?"

"This is it. Nobody here but the military and us."

"*Nobody*?"

"Yep, we got it all to ourselves. Look, there's where the Kingsway used to be."

"Oh, look at that! I heard about it being hit, but—"

Just then, bright lights come on us from both sides of the road, and a soldier with a rifle pointing at us is standing in the middle of the road screaming, "Halt! Halt!"

"Shit! Shit!" I cry out, and Ralph slams on his brakes, while shouting, "Red Cross! Red Cross!"

Gabriel clutches my arm. The soldier shuts up long enough to hear Ralph identify us, and we are allowed to pass. Benjamin, in the front seat, laughs nervously, then we all laugh, and all of us swear, some in English, some in Yoruba, some in both.

"Welcome to Port Harcourt, guys!" Ralph says and beats his hand on the steering wheel.

Gabriel lets go of my arm. It is only then that I notice it hurts where he grabbed me. "Are there any more of those?"

"You never know. They keep changing them. There's usually one back there. That's a big intersection." He gestures over his shoulder. "That road there leads to the wharf."

"I know," I say.

"Been here before?"

"I was a Peace Corps Volunteer near here until just after the war started. I was here when it was Nigeria the *first* time and when it became Biafra."

"Teacher?"

"Yeah. We saw the school on the way in. I think it had been bombed."

"Probably. Everything has been."

Ahead, there were lights, and we brace for another sudden screaming, gun-wielding soldier. Instead, the roadblock is civilized, the solder calmly holds up his hand, and comes to the driver's window. "Good evening, Mistah Red Cross Man," the soldier says. The bayonet glistens in the lights.

Ralph parks near the doorway to an apartment building, and hustles us and the trunks up the stairs.

Dr. Martin is an Indian who is much blacker than any Nigerian I have ever seen. He is wearing a white tropical shirt and black slacks and holding a drink. He does not look friendly.

"Keep away from the windows," is the first thing he says. No hello. No smile. His accent is more British than anything else. "Don't leave here and don't look out the windows. You'll be back at the airport tomorrow morning. Back to Lagos!" Then he turns and walks to the kitchen. "Shall we go eat?" Women emerge from the doorway.

"We'll introduce ourselves when we get back from dinner," one of them says. Like Ralph, she has a strong American accent. "There's food in the refrigerator. Help yourselves. Just don't eat the Jell-O salad. That's for tomorrow. On Sundays we skip mess hall food."

Dr. Martin puts his drink down on a small table by the door. "Remember, keep away from the windows!" The three of us barely wait until they have left before we collapse in a fit of giggles. I cover my mouth with a pillow.

Benjamin stands in front of us, folds his arms in an exaggerated manner, and frowns deeply. "The windows!" he says with an affected British accent. "The windows!"

Gabriel laughs so hard he falls off the couch onto the floor.

The dark curtains are closed. I have an insane urge to tear them open, and cry, "Viva Biafra!" We hear noises of vehicles coming and going and people shouting greetings and orders to one another.

The refrigerator yields some canned food which we eat cold, none of us up to using the strange stove, and we are almost asleep on the sofas when the group returns.

Dr. Martin has calmed down and questions us intensely about our orders. He is satisfied that we did what Bulle wanted us to. Ralph, it turns out, is a jack-of-all-trades for this medical team, and the women are nurses. They are Lutherans. Even Dr. Martin is a Lutheran. And a Canadian citizen. The more we learn about him, the odder the combination of things becomes.

Apparently, the Lutherans have had missions here for a long time, although I can't recall ever having heard of them. My previous Nigerian experience drenched me in Catholicism.

They speak as if we are not present, discussing plans, work schedules and personalities that mean nothing to us. Finally, we are given places to sleep.

✤ ✤ ✤

The red-and-white Cessna lifts easily into the sky and arcs itself towards the west in a drastic contrast to the flight yesterday. We are the only passengers, and we sit silently, looking down as the sea crashes against the coast of Africa. I wonder, when we are first aloft, what is Nigeria and what is Biafra as I look to the north. From here, it all looks so peaceful, so much alike, palm trees leading into more palm trees. You would never suspect there is a war going on down there, and that people are dying, or that people you know are hiding in among those very palm trees, hiding from others, some of whom you also know. It is the first time the war has seemed just this unreal.

✤ ✤ ✤

Dr. Bulle answers the door to his small apartment. "Good God—" he cries out. As briefly as I can, I explain our adventures and tell him that we must have prior written permission the next time. He begins to laugh halfway through my stories, and is still laughing when I finish.

I want to hit him and knock him across the bed.

Our living quarters in Elele. My bedroom was directly above the Red Cross banner.

The drums contained gasoline that I had to siphon by mouth to fill the two Land Rovers. Medicine was stored in the building behind the gasoline barrels.

Each day of the week, we set up a clinic and feeding station in a different village. The mixture of corn, soya beans, and meal ("CSM") was the most nutritious food we could provide. Col. Adekunle had his soldiers paint over "The International Committee of" on all our vehicles, leaving only "The Red Cross."

Several thousand people were fed and treated every day at our clinics.

While such wartime photos of nude or semi-nude children with distended stomachs were disturbing to many who saw them, these children were actually far better off than those suffering from kwashiorkor. They could stand up, walk, and smile.

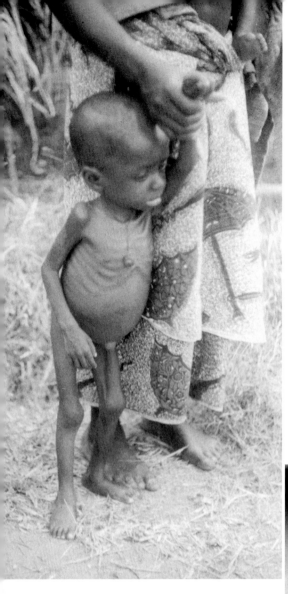

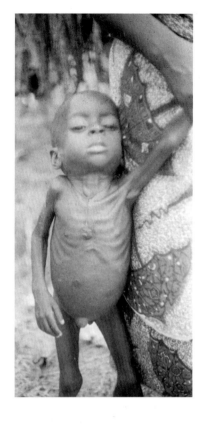

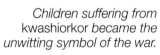

Children suffering from kwashiorkor *became the unwitting symbol of the war.*

The women waited in lines for hours to get food for their families.

Biafran currency and stamps
replaced Nigerian versions, only
to be replaced once again when
the front lines shifted.

Daily Flash

A ROCKWELL PUBLICATION

SATURDAY JULY 15 1967

Free. Frank. Fearless

TWO PENCE

VOL 1 NO. 183

CURE YOUR
PRINTING
HEADACHES
PHONE 8294
ROCKWELL LIMITED
6 & 19 Accra Street
P. O. Box 918
Port Harcourt
for
Specialist Printing

BIAFRANS BE VIGILANT!

BIAFRAN AIR FORC
STRIKES AGAIN

Saudi Arabia's oil blockade still on

SAUDI Arabia Minister for Oil, said Ahmad Yamani has emphasised that his country has no intention of lifting the oil blockade against the United States, Britain and West Germany.

The oil blockade was imposed by a conference of oil producing countries in Kuwait early last month following the Arab-Israeli war.

Said Ahmad who is now visiting Kuwait was re-buffing charges made by the IAP Council

Nigerian Troops Vanquished

BIAFRAN troops in the current war between Nigeria and Biafra have continued to give good account of themselves at the war front and the Nigerian invaders are suffering terrible setback not only because they cannot find ready answers to the manoeuvres of their superior Biafran counterparts but also because of imminent shortage of essential supplies required for war.

The Biafran Defence Headquarters in a release last night disclosed that the Biafran Air Force, despite unfavourable weather yesterday continued its daily raid behind the frontlines of the Nigerian

of attrition by Biafran troops.

In the north-east front the enemy, as has been expected, entered Ogoja town yesterday but their advance has been halted, it said, adding that Biafra

One of the measures adopted by Yakubu Gowon towards averting petrol shortage was to introduce petrol rationing by a decree. A decree issued by Gowon yesterday and published to take immediate effect empowers his government to control the storage, transportation and distribution of petroleum products throughout the country.

It also says government will take over by force any firm which refuses

its order to rationing off.

It also ca vernment with storage store pet failure to this orde result to over the

Also seize oil oil prospe company refuses a spec crude o

PUBLIC NO

Guardian

THAT UNIVERSAL BROTHERHOOD SHALL BECOME A REALITY

VOL XXVII NO. 9,396   THURSDAY   JUNE 1 1967   PRICE   TWO PENCE

ANTI-BIAFRA CAMPAIGN
ABORTIVE

Amend pools law call

ABA, May 31.—The Government of Biafra has been urged to amend the country's Pool Law. Making the call yesterday, Mr S. E. Oni-kanma, a pool agent said the present pools law in the country was an imitation of the Nigeria law.

The law he said, afforded the pools promoters the opportunity of cheating stakers who win weekly on fixed odds.

ENUGU, May 31—All ships that call at the ports of the Biafra Republic have been guaranteed of safety.

The Biafra Marketing Board in a statement here today said that it had come to its notice that the Nigerian Marketing Company Limited to now resorted to issuing threats propagating falsehood to foreign shipping companies in continuation of its bid to isolate and strangulate the Republic of Biafra economically.

The Biafra Marketing Board warned that it is impossible for the Nigerian Produce Marketing Company Limited to interfere with the normal movement of vessels

Marketing Board, the Nigerian Government must have discovered that its campaigns in European capitals to dissuade foreign shipping companies from sending their ships to Biafra ports have not only proved abortive but have been soundly condemned by the outside world

stuff which has already proved to be a disastrous failure as can be attested to by local representatives of foreign shipping companies

It then re-emphasised

PH ULC greets Ojukwu

The United Labour Congress, Port Harcourt, has congratulated the Military Governor on the proclamation of

Neither the Nigerian nor the Biafran media showed any objectivity in the coverage of the war—or in the months preceding secession.

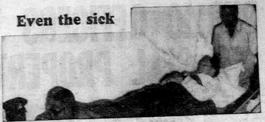

Daily Times

THE INDEPENDENT NEWSPAPER

●18,396 Saturday, July 22, 1967 3d

Even the sick

580 FOREIGNERS SAIL IN

By FEMI SONAIKE and PETER OLAFIOYE

FOREIGNERS deserting the three states in the former Eastern Region arrived in Lagos last night with stories of hardship and soaring prices in the East.

A Phillipino medical practitioner, recalling his experiences in Enugu in the past two months said: "Life was terrible, we were treated roughly like criminals and shouted down as saboteurs."

The practitioner was sure "the economy of the rebels" will fall in another month.

"Before I left, salt was selling at 2s a cup. Most offices have been closed down and many workers sat idle reading newspapers," the doctor said.

Waving aside as "mere propaganda" Ojukwu's claim that he was according still resistance to Federal troops, the medical practitioner said the rebels "are in panic and confusion."

In the hospital where he worked, the doctor said there was an acute shortage of medicine.

Materials

The doctor hoped to proceed to his home country during the week-end.

Evacuees from the East

Lec REFRIGERATORS

"580 Foreigners Sail In" announced our arrival in Lagos from Port Harcourt.

CURE YOUR PRINTING HEADACHES

ROCKWELL LIMITED PHONE 8294
8 & 10 Accra Street
P O Box 914
Port Harcourt

for Specialist Printing

Daily Flash
A ROCKWELL PUBLICATION

VOL 1 NO 177 SATURDAY JULY 1 1967 TWO PENCE

BIAFRAN TROOPS REPULSE NIGERIAN INVASION

Life And Death Struggle With Nigeria

THE Head of State and Military Governor of the Republic of Biafra, Lt. Col. Ojukwu has said that the victory of Biafra over Nigeria which will be assured by God would immortalise the memory of Biafrans who were ignominously murdered by Northern Nigerians.

This is contained in a message which Governor Ojukwu sent to Mrs Florence Okoro, on the occasion of the first anniversary of the death of her husband, Lt. Col. Okoro.

Biafrans by Northern Nigerians Biafrans are currently engaged in a life and death struggle with Nigeria.

Ikwerre—Etche donates further £1,000

AN additional amount of over £1,000 was donated yesterday by Communities, Individuals and Organisations in Ikwerre/Etche Division towards the Civil Defence Fund.

Whole Company 6 Officers Killed

NIGERIA has attacked Biafra. The enemy offensives, led by white mercenaries were launched on Biafran troops positioned at Daken, Obodu, Ninya and Enugu/Ezeike areas in Ogoja and Nsukka Provinces.

Reports from the battle front showed that Biafran troops repelled the enemy's attack forcing them to retreat with heavy casualties.

Fighting with heavy mortar, the Biafran troops moved down the Nigerian troops pushing them back to mark their five miles inside the Northern Nigeria territory.

As the time of our last report the Biafran troops receiving treatment in Biafran hospitals.

An Army Bulletin issued yesterday said although fighting was still on in the Nsukka area of Ogoja border, the enemy had not been able to break through.

At the Ogoja sector anywhere pointed out, the enemy had been completely silenced. Most of the civilians living along the

YIKKERS SATURDAY

Your stay was indeed good and we have been anxious to see you around what my Hakkies or the only that as professional help that as professional help
— The Biafteer

Hundreds of thousands of "Safe Conduct Pass" leaflets—printed in English and three Nigerian languages—were dropped by air over Biafra by the Nigerians.

A woodcut of Lt. Col. Odumegwu Ojukwu, the leader of Biafra.

THE REPUBLIC OF BIAFRA

LT. COL. ODUMEGWU OJUKWU.

THE BIAFRA NATIONAL ANTHEM

```
: m | r m | f :-|- : m | r : m | d :- : r| r:m |- : -|-
: m | r m | f :-|- : m | r : m | d :- : r| m:- |- :-|-
: s | s : s | l :-|- : m | m : s  s :- : r| r:f |- : -|-
: f | m:r | m:- |- : d { d : r| r :- : m | m:- |- : -|-
: s | s : s | l :-|- : m | m : s | s :- : r| r:f |- : -|
: f | m : r | m:- |- : d { d : r| r :- d { d :- |- : - -|-
```

```
f | m |
d | d |
l | s |
f | d |
```
Amen.

WORDS

"The Biafran National Anthem" used these words set to the music of "Finlandia" by Sibelius. It was first played on all Biafran radio stations the morning of secession, May 30, 1967.

REPUBLIC OF BIAFRA

30TH MAY 1967.

The Rising Sun was the symbol of Biafra and appeared, among other places, on shoulder patches on military uniforms.

Opinion was often expressed in chalk on the walls of buildings.

This poster was found on a door in an abandoned school. "Biafra" is being subdued by the "Enemy," depicted as Nigerian Muslims under the control of Europeans.

"Ojukwu keep off Nigeria already take over" warned the Biafran leader to stay away from the parts of Biafra that were back in Nigerian hands. "To keep Nigeria one is a task that must be done" was an anti-secessionist slogan frequently seen and heard in Nigeria.

Inga Brunne and Olive Dempsey, both nurses, and Dr. Brace Hintz are shown taking a lunch break at one of the clinics.

Inga (shown in white headband) dispensed medicine from a table set up under a tree.

Brace waited for the Nigerian military and civilians to clear the roads so we could go to our clinic for the day. The trees had been cut down as an act of sabotage by Biafrans hiding near Elele.

All photos by John Sherr

One of the refugees in the former prison at Owerri where we conducted a clinic for a weeks until Owerri was once again in Biafran hands. The photo was taken from the ro where we were dispensing medicine, looking into the courtyard of the building.

NOVEMBER 1968 – ELELE

The bugs and I are struggling for the light of this small kerosene lantern. I have been in my bedroom only minutes, and already my ankles itch from mosquito bites. A spider is slowly making a net on some shelves above me.

The medicines are again packed tightly in their boxes in the trunks, which are locked safely downstairs. We'll load them in the morning. Everything else is tucked in the Land Rovers. The used syringes that we emptied today have been broken and are now buried out back.

Olive is driving south to P.H. in the morning for more medicines. Because the roads are so horrible, the 35 miles will probably take her two hours. Inga, Brace and I will carry on at the clinic until she gets back.

All of us—soldiers, civilians, relief workers—are bugs caught in a spider's net. It is not a question of being devoured; it is a question of how *soon* one will be consumed.

✦ ✦ ✦

Olive Dempsey is an American nurse, Inga Brunne a Danish nurse, and Brace Hintz an American doctor. They are all Lutherans, forming a medical team sponsored by the Lutheran Church—Missouri Synod. Dr. Bulle is Missouri Synod, too. Until a few weeks ago, I had never heard of the Missouri Synod and now I'm part of their team, based in Elele, 35 miles north of Port Harcourt. Inga, who spent years in the Northern Region at a hospital, speaks Hausa well enough to converse with the occasional soldier. Olive, a widow, had retired, was living in California, and was glad to be offered the chance to be busy again. She got her wish! Brace was in practice in Wisconsin. And then there's me, bouncing around Africa like an out-of-control ball, about as un-medical and un-Lutheran as one can get.

+ + +

I hear a plane going over. It sounds quite low. I wonder if it's a Nigerian military plane or a relief flight into Biafra. I almost think, "Is it ours or theirs?" Ours. Theirs. How can I think "ours" or "theirs" in this conflict?

+ + +

The soldiers here are angry. The Biafrans come into Elele at night to harass them; sometimes a soldier is shot, perhaps even killed. It seems as if it's done in a pixieish way, almost for fun. The marauders may not be Biafran soldiers, at all, but Biafran civilians who keep up a psychological war of nerves. If I'm ever going to fight in a war like this one, I want to be the defender of the turf, the guerrilla. The Nigerians don't like being the Hessians.

+ + +

I stood in my doorway, as the shadows began their stretching out from the main classroom block, moving slowly, darkly across the playing field. In front of me, on the driveway, were the fourth-form and fifth-form boys, marching smartly with wooden sticks for rifles. They were being led by one of the tutors who had spent some short amount of time in the army. They were counting off, "One! Two! Three! Four!"

Preparations for war had come to the school. Suddenly, the tutor halted the boys and I saw some of them wiping dust off their sandals, straightening their shirt collars, looking at their watches. They appeared bored, annoyed at being dirtied and made to perspire in their school clothes.

That evening, I had trouble getting to sleep.

+ + +

This house belongs to a lawyer who is now a prisoner of the Biafrans. His son helps as an interpreter here at our clinic in Elele. It is odd to have him sit down as our guest in the living room of his own house. When the Nigerians were about to take over Elele, this boy was the only one of his family who was willing to hide. The others disappeared. He doesn't know if they're prisoners of the Nigerians or of the Biafrans, or if they fled with the retreating Biafrans. We don't speak to him of the possibility they all got machine-gunned down in the mob scene when the one side was fleeing and the other advancing.

+ + +

If that is one of the Biafran planes (one rarely hears "Biafra" used here; instead, it is "the rebels"), it no doubt is taking medicine and food in for the starving kids. We see a lot of children suffering here, too, but not nearly so much as there. But the rest of the world is seeing photos only of the Biafran kids who are dying, not the Nigerian ones who are dying too.

+ + +

I force-feed some medicine down a little girl's throat. I feel so guilty. I have to squeeze hard against the jaws with my fingers, and make the mouth come open. The child is silent—they almost always are—but she resists my efforts with an amazing show of strength, or maybe I am not as forceful as I might be. The medicine goes down, the child chokes, then swallows it. Her mother has been yelling at her to take it, but her heart isn't in it, either. We stare at one another over the girl's head. I have to ask Peter, our interpreter at this particular village, to tell the woman to quiet down, as I can't stand her shrill voice right in my ear. That medicine down her unwilling throat, together with other medicine, an injection, a bar of brown soap for her scabies, and a bag of the combination of corn, soya beans, and meal, might make that kid live long enough for us to get back to her next week. Might.

+ + +

They don't smile. I think that bothers me more than anything. They sit on the wooden benches in the converted schoolrooms and stare. They don't sleep. They just gaze across the room. At first, I tickled them under the chin, or made a face, or said something in my Pidgin Igbo until I realized there would be no response, child after child. They remind me of very old, very ill people who lie on their beds week after week. Most of them are naked; their bellies are bloated, their ankles are swollen with edema and their skin has a reddish-whitish cast to it. The hair is a giveaway too. It's never black, but always a reddish-blond— one more tell-tale sign of malnutrition. I have come to hate it. Sometimes the skin is pulled back on the face in a way that gives them a macabre smile. It makes one want to flee. I do not have nightmares about them, perhaps because my mind knows I will see them, or another group just like them, the next day.

✛　✛　✛

It is a shock to work with Nigerians who don't speak English. I am so accustomed to dealing with people who have at least some education. Now, I see almost no one but shy grandmothers who giggle at me, and who rattle off a loud Igbo in my ear, or young women with absolutely no formal education whose husbands, if they are the ones who speak English, are now in hiding, or in the 'rebel' army, or already dead.

We are told the educated ones have been forced to flee with the Biafrans. Brace thinks it's because the Biafran government, with the help of the Biafran soldiers, takes them along to run that very government infrastructure. Olive prefers the theory that the Biafrans need them for a public-relations reason: If the educated ones, presumably the smart ones, are sticking with Biafra, it makes that side look good. It's probably both reasons, plus the fact that the educated ones, like a lot of the uneducated ones, are convinced they'll be killed by the Nigerians if they don't stay inside a shrinking Biafra.

✛　✛　✛

We saw more than 700 people today in the clinic. And provided food for more than 15,000.

Brace remains startled at the dried fish, the whole fish body flat and hard, and a ghastly thing to smell.

"I know it's wonderful as a source of protein," he says to me, "but—ugh!"

"Surely you've seen worse. After all, you're a doctor," I reply.

"I never had a patient that looked that bad."

"Or smelled that bad?"

"Yes, thank the Lord, or smelled that bad."

✢　✢　✢

"Don't eat that," my student said to me, as we sat with his adult male relatives around a platter of tiny, whole fish covered with an orange pepper sauce.

"It's OK," I replied, certain that I was by now conditioned to the hot food that has been such a shock to my system. He looked at me, perplexed.

After the fish had burned my tongue and lips, enough to make my eyes water and cause me to have a coughing fit, I attempted to stick my tongue into the beer, trying to soothe it.

I-told-you-so looks are universal.

✢　✢　✢

While we are setting up the trays and making sure we have enough benches and so forth, Olive walks into the crowd of thousands of people and hands out cards that allow those persons to be seen either by Brace or her. Olive, a nurse, acts like a doctor, and I, a civilian, act like a pharmacist. Inga does both nursing and dispensing, but sometimes she too sees patients, and I dispense alone.

The people pinch and poke Olive, and many yell at her, with high-pitched voices, inadvertently spitting on her, in order to try to get a card. The most ill, ironically, make little noise, but Olive looks for them, often on the edge of the crowd, and presses cards into the mothers' hands, and sometimes even escorts the most ill right to Brace; then she goes out to face the crowds again. I think she dreams of California.

✢　✢　✢

They come to Inga and me with their little slips of paper with the prescriptions written on them. We stand across from one another and reach into the various cubbyholes of the trays to search out the medicines that Brace and Olive tell us to give them. Sometimes, Brace will write a cryptic note, a humorous aside, on a paper and we'll have a small joke to talk about when we take our lunch breaks, or later in the day after we've returned and are filling up the trays once again.

Inga, being Danish, doesn't always catch the idiomatic English of Brace's jokes, so I spend time, while I am filling up a little vial of some life-giving substance, explaining some Americanism.

It is ironic that I, who could barely pass biology, am now diagnosing *kwashiorkor* in little children in a country I knew only from my stamp collection and acting as pharmacist hundreds of times a day. At first, they also wanted me to give injections, but they decided against it, to my obvious relief. When I'm not dispensing medicine, I clean wounds for Olive or Inga to dress; feed kids the supplements we cook up; clean ears and mouths; help the Nigerian Red Cross guys set up their food-distribution lines; and run any number of errands.

When we arrive at the clinics, lines have already formed for the food and the medicine. We serve hundreds a day and many cannot be seen until late in the afternoon.

✛　✛　✛

We rise at 7. I shave with cold water dipped out of a bucket. The toilet works because we pour water into the tank of the commode. Very Peace Corps-ish.

✛　✛　✛

The soldier, one I've seen before, smiles at me when we pull up to the ex-post office in Elele to load up our supplies. "Give me ride to clinic," he says, and I nod my head.

We are full, so he sits on the left fender, his gun across his lap. It is only while we are heading down the road that I realize how bad this looks. I do not like to blow my horn at the people in the road for fear I will startle them. The soldier bangs on the hood; when that, and the sound of the motor, get the attention of the people, they turn round. It is then that he waves his gun in the air, and scares them off the roadway.

I bang on the window to get him to stop, but he can't hear me over the noise of the motor and the people shouting; besides, he is too busy yelling and keeping up a rapid conversation in Pidgin with everyone. God, how stupid of me. Here I am, a keeper of the peace, with an armed soldier on the front of my vehicle.

I am even afraid to stop, for fear he will fall off and his gun discharge. So we continue down the road, the soldier frightening the people who are coming to see us today.

This will be talked about around the campfires in Elele tonight. "The young white man," one of them will say. "Did you see him today? He was carrying one of the soldiers on the front of his vehicle."

"Idiot!" one of the others will reply. "Doesn't that man have any sense? He could have gotten us killed! White people!"

I should be the last to forget that I live in a fishbowl. Everything I do is noticed, everything I say is remembered and repeated. There is no way I can blend into this town or this country with the color of my skin and the addition of white vehicles with big red crosses on them.

Write down 100 times: "I am an *onye ocha*. Everybody knows what I do, what I say, what I wear, where I go. Everybody."

Fortunately, today, Brace doesn't see my armed accompaniment or I might be in for a stern lecture.

✦ ✦ ✦

I became accustomed to someone I had never seen before coming up to me at a bus stop or in the market in Eleme and saying, "You're the teacher at the secondary school, aren't you." Not a question, they were so sure they are right. At first, I was amazed that they knew who I was. Everywhere I went within five miles, ten miles, people addressed me as "Teacher" or, sometimes, "Piss Cup!" We called ourselves Piss Cup Volunteers, which took on new meaning when we had to, once again, provide specimens to the Piss Cup doctor and nurse.

✦ ✦ ✦

I give cooking demonstrations at each of the six villages we now serve. I mix some corn-soya bean-meal mixture with water, then cook it in a pot over the fire. We are trying to convince these people to eat something that is a perfect food for their present conditions—but which is unfamiliar to them. Large crowds gather to see what this white man is about to do, and they stay for my talk, translated into their particular Igbo dialect.

✦ ✦ ✦

A woman is caught stuffing medicine into her mouth, medicine that we have just given her for her baby. I am aghast. That's one reason we administer as much medicine as possible to the kids when they are on the benches in front of us.

✦ ✦ ✦

On the day we were being evacuated from Biafra, an enormously fat man in a big American car pulled up to the hotel. There were three others in the car. Two were with him, but he seemed to be the only one who had a gun. The fourth man was tied up and sat alone in the back seat. He was someone they had "captured." It was not clear what his crime was, or even if he were guilty of anything. The war had been on for one week.

"Traitor!" the fat man shouted, and looked at us for our reaction. We were afraid to react. We had seen the confusion and the fear at the roadblocks, when people who knew us were suddenly armed militia who shouted at us to identify ourselves and admit whether or not we were mercenaries. We gave the fat man no visible reaction, but stood mute. Am I destined to stand mute through all of this?

✦ ✦ ✦

Adekunle apparently stayed in the priests' house at my old school when his soldiers occupied the compound. So odd, I can hardly imagine the scene.

✦ ✦ ✦

We have a run on a case of new glass bottles. The women find out we have them and they all get rid of the ones they brought. It's just as well. Most of the ones they bring are so filthy we can't use them. And there's no place to send the women to wash the bottles if they aren't useable. We give out more bottles than we expect to, but we can be comforted by the fact that the liquid medicine goes home in clean bottles.

✛ ✛ ✛

The mosquitoes seem to have quieted down. My ankles are a bunch of welts and I find myself scratching them again and again. I have been faithful in taking my Aralen; I can't afford to get malaria. I don't think Brace would let me sleep in even for one day if I had it, and I could hardly do that anyway when probably half the people we see are suffering from it, on top of all their other illnesses.

✛ ✛ ✛

I was sitting in someone's apartment in Port Harcourt, hours before we were to be evacuated. The boys, all Ibos, were talking about the war that is now upon us. After bravado, talk of a quick, decisive win, they turned their attention to those in Biafra who were not Ibo. "Rivers!" said one boy, wrinkling his nose. "We'll take care of the Rivers people as soon as we have won this war! Just wait!" he said, loudly, to no one in particular.

✛ ✛ ✛

A teenage boy, one of our interpreters, tells me that he had decided not to flee when the Nigerians were about to take Elele because, if he were going to die, "I'm going to die in my papa-land." In the newly liberated villages, we rarely see males between the ages of, say, 13 and 40. It is a dangerous age. They're suspected by both sides of being spies and/or soldiers for the other side, and, if the front lines change suddenly, as they do sometimes, they are caught in a trap where they will likely be killed by the conquerors. And the insistence of the group that takes over that this boy or that man is a danger is contagious, and crowds form and people begin to shout, and suddenly shots ring out and one more person dies. Another innocent. Bang! Just like that.

✛ ✛ ✛

The crowd is stampeding, trying to rush the doors to get their food. Their own villagers, some of the few young men still around, are beating at them with sticks. Everyone is shouting, and the dust is blinding us to some of the melee. It takes precious minutes, sometimes half an hour, to get the people back in line. For reasons that are unclear, the old women seem to be the instigators of these instant panics. Perhaps they fear they won't get any food this time, or they see a neighbor getting food first, maybe someone younger than they are, and their sense of status is offended.

✛ ✛ ✛

One man is found with six ration tickets instead of the allotted number: one. They are apparently for sale for 3*d* or 6*d*. At least there are no facilities available for counterfeiting them or I don't know what we'd do. Can one blame people for greed in the light of what they have gone through and are continuing to go through? If most of one's children and grandchildren have died or disappeared and one is continually hungry, is there any reason one wouldn't cheat to get a little more for those who are left?

Then, in moments of anger, I lash out at the injustice of anyone taking more than one's share when so many around us can barely survive from week to week on what we can spare for them. I want to be somewhere where my values aren't tested quite so sharply, where morals aren't strung out like a tight rubber band while we all wait for it to snap. Sometimes I look out from the table where we are dispensing feverishly and see Olive trying to make her way through the noisy crowds and then spy a child in someone's arms bobbing around with that too-familiar look of *kwashiorkor* and I suddenly want, if only for a day, a ranch-style house in a complacent suburb where one's social problems consist of whom to invite over for steaks this Saturday. Just one day, God.

✛ ✛ ✛

I threaten to send one woman out if she will not keep quiet and stop trying to get ahead of the others in the line. Her child looks no worse than those ahead of her do. We will never know what old animosities are here; whether, for example, she has always hated the three women in front of her on the bench. The interpreters are reluctant to take the women on sometimes, and I can't say that I blame them, but I do it willingly, partly because I can yell at them and get rid of some of my own frustration, partly because someone needs to yell at them to try to bring them to their senses, and partly because I will go away and not have to live with them for the rest of my life.

+ + +

"The soldiers have discovered that these villagers built roadblocks back in the bush," says Brace.

"Whatever for?" I am puzzled.

"To keep the refugees out. They don't want them coming into their villages seeking help."

"Oh, for chrissakes."

+ + +

On the front of our house is a large Red Cross banner. I think too often of Save-the-Children Charlie's teasing reminder that this will help "them" aim better. He's right. A mortar aimed at the banner would go right through my bedroom. Hell, right through *me*.

+ + +

The child is screaming. It is my white face again. What must I look like to a child who has never seen anyone who wasn't black or brown? I have a ghost face and long, ghost arms reaching for the child and I speak a strange ghost language. They will sit in the laps or the arms and not notice anything, and then suddenly I put my hand to their faces and turn their heads towards me. Perhaps they think it is they who have died.

He pees on my foot. It is the second time today that has happened. His mother is screaming at him to take his medicine, to stop screaming, to open his mouth. I tell the interpreter to make the mother be quiet. She quiets, and then the child quiets. Until I go to pour the cup of medicine into his mouth. The mother doesn't scream this time, but holds tightly onto the frail bony body. I am startled by the other interpreter who splashes water on my foot. I nod my thanks and then raise the cup to the child's lips.

He pees on me again.

✛ ✛ ✛

I feel very disturbed, very odd. Even with my experiences in Lagos with the wounded soldiers and the *Doppelgänger* at the nightclub, I have a conflict within myself regarding the soldiers here when we give them medical treatment. I want to say to them to go away and get themselves to a military hospital. And then I feel very ashamed. Does a human being remain a human being when he dresses in army green? We do not treat the average complaints, only those which require immediate attention, but for some reason I have given a purity to the civilian that I deny the military man. I am so mixed up. Many of the soldiers are so young they are the age of my former students. And the Biafrans are supposed to be even younger. A war of boys fighting men's grievances. Villagers fleeing bombs. Vietnam.

✛ ✛ ✛

I am getting a headache from driving over these roads. The Biafrans bulldozed huge holes in them to slow down the Nigerian advance, and placed mines in some of them, or felled huge trees across the roads. The Nigerians cut the trees in pieces and pulled them to the sides of the roads, and filled in the holes with sand and dirt. And the roads were nothing to brag about even before the war. We bump along, slowed down in our efforts to go in any direction from Elele. My headache gets worse.

✛ ✛ ✛

"Damn!" I cried out. "Aaah!" cried my student. The lorry driver seemed to hit every chuckhole possible. We were facing backwards, our legs dangling from the board we were sitting on. The board, too, flew into the air every time we hit a hole. At first it was fun, then it became annoying and I wondered how sore I would be in the morning. We each held tightly onto metal poles rising from the sides of the lorry as we, the board, and our asses

rose into the air, again and again. Women with large bundles of firewood saw us as we drove by. The sight of a white man hitchhiking was novel enough for them to stop, cry out, and seize their loads tightly as they began to laugh and point with their free hands. "Eeeee, onye ocha!"

Thirty miles never, never seemed so long before.

✤ ✤ ✤

The old women have this belief that injections work, but pills or liquid medicines don't. They come up to us, peck us hard with their bony fingers, and demand injections. We and the interpreters shoo them out and the interpreters laugh. If the women see them laughing, they go on a rampage. We have to evict them bodily from the pharmacy area sometimes. Everything about them seems tough, including their skin, which is leathery and shiny and hugs their bones. When they laugh, it is marvelous. Their mouths are often toothless, and there is a sparkle to their eyes, and the effect of their faces thrown back in a good, high-pitched laugh is infectious.

✤ ✤ ✤

Col. Henshaw, who is in charge of the troops in the Elele area, has a brother fighting for Biafra. It's a perfect civil war.

✤ ✤ ✤

We were sitting on the grass between my house and Amadi's. Palm wine flowed among the teachers at the end of another school day. The radio set reported loud and clear what was happening in the nation's capital and the regional capitals. No one doubted that the affairs were coming to a head. Government officials were posturing, proclaiming their innocence, denouncing the other side. We listened without comment for most of the broadcast, quietly sipping our glasses of palm wine. Almost in a singing voice, a wail, Okeke summed up the news reporting with, "O, Nigeria!" The "O" was long, drawn-out, fatalistic. A High Life song came on and one of the men got up and danced. We laughed, but no one cheered him on as we usually did.

The old man insists on being helped ahead of a benchful of children and we are all angry. "Go away!" I shout, and wave the pen in my hand at him. He stamps his cane and cries out in this village's particular Igbo dialect that he has a right to be served. Is he not old? Is not age respected? These others are *pekins*, only a few years old. He is tired, he is sore, he needs medicines to get well, he has grown weary of this war and its dislocation of everything. I want some snuff, he cries. Give me some gin, even a little. Serve me, he cries, serve me. I don't want to wait in line. I must not wait in line. He stamps his cane again. The interpreter helping Inga turns him forcibly and steers him roughly out of our area. If it is a typical day, he will be back.

✛   ✛   ✛

I do not write home what I am thinking about, nor can I say very much about the day-to-day work. I do not mention front lines, troop movements, etc. although we know pretty well what they are. It is very interesting being forced to be neutral in a conflict in which I have such personal concerns; having friends on both sides helps keep that neutrality. Any bomb, any bullet could hit someone I know. Our knowledge of the war makes us disdain the reports printed in the world press; we forgive the Biafran radio and the Nigerian newspapers—they are expected to lie, to exaggerate, to puff up and tear down. But the others are not privy to information that we are, and it gives me a strange feeling of superiority. And often when they do report something, it is misspelled, or it is simply incorrect, or assumptions and editorial stances are, to us, odd.

My aerogrammes contain no name, no return address. I write every letter imagining it on the front page of some Lagos daily.

✛   ✛   ✛

I am carrying a dead baby. I have never done this before. Last night, the woman stayed in this house with her baby on an I-V. Brace insisted on sleeping downstairs near them so he could be awakened if anything was wrong. Olive wanted to take his place, but he said no. The baby lived through the night, but this morning while we were getting dressed, it died. The mother cried out when Brace confirmed what she feared. The other three arranged to go to our clinic today in the one Land Rover and I am assigned the task of taking her and the baby near her village.

Brace is very specific. I am not to take her all the way home. She lives about four miles off the main road and he is afraid there might be Biafrans, or even deserting Nigerians, who will take the vehicle and who might bump me off in the process. I don't think that is likely since it is stark white with large red crosses on all four sides and even on the roof. But when I mention that, it doesn't faze him. He mentions land mines on the dirt road as another possibility, and that convinces me, finally, that I must not drive the extra few miles.

I take the baby from the cot. It reminds me of picking up a piece of Styrofoam for the first time. Your arms go up sharply when they are confronted with a lot less weight than they were expecting. The mother gathers her few belongings while I hold the baby and follow her outside. I am glad to be able to hand it over to her when she is quietly sitting on the front seat. A cruel irony is here. The baby's surprisingly light weight comes to me in comparative images: Baked egg whites. Meringue. Food. Nothing but food.

✦ ✦ ✦

We ride in silence. I had never noticed before that the keys banged so hard against the steering column. I hear everything. The shifting of gears. The wooden boxes in the back of the van sliding into one another. I imagine I hear the child breathing.

I pull off the paved main road and stop at the beginning of the dirt road leading to her village. She looks at me in alarm and surprise. I explain what Brace has told me and say I have been given strict orders. She shakes her head and protests. "I can't," I say, and feel my cheeks grow hot. She doesn't understand what I mean by land mines and keeps assuring me that there are no soldiers from either side anywhere near her village. Finally, she picks up her small maroon purse, opens the door, and steps down. The baby is held tightly to her chest. I quietly say, "Good-bye" and "I'm sorry." She doesn't answer. I sit there until the first curve of the road takes her out of my sight and then I pack up and drive to join the others at the clinic. Brace's first words are,

"Did you stop just off the road?" and I say, rather sharply, that I did. I hate him for asking that.

The child is probably buried already. And that woman will never forget that I refused to take her to her village.

All of this is making me a little insane.

DECEMBER 1968 – OWERRI 5

The rockets hitting the earth are making the glass bottles rattle. Michael, one of the Nigerian Red Cross men, looks as if he is about to run. Inga and I trade glances every once in a while and keep up our morbid, rapid-fire exchange of jokes about the whole situation.

"Did you know they sang 'Nearer My God to Thee' as the *Titanic* was sinking?" I ask her, and she smiles.

"But it didn't work! Quick! Think of another hymn." I am once again amused by her dry wit in her second language. She has taught me greetings in Danish, and a couple of "not very nice" words too, but she won't translate them for me.

There is a close one. One bottle that we didn't realize was so near the edge falls off, and Inga grabs it just in time. We take a moment to rearrange the boxes.

We can hear the Biafran guns going akk-akk-akk, the infamous AK-47s, we assume. The Biafrans are determined to get Owerri back. The front is very near.

Michael moves closer to the table when another rocket goes off. He is almost finished putting tablets into little white envelopes.

We are treating "real" Ibos this time, not Rivers area people who use an Igbo dialect; I look even harder at them to see if I recognize any. It is difficult to tell, as some of the faces are so gaunt and so many of the people merely stare ahead and do not recognize anything. If these people should survive the war, there will be so many of them who will be mentally ill from the strains of the war and the lack of the right kinds of food for so long. And it's far worse with the children.

✛   ✛   ✛

It is an odd situation. These people inside the prison are from this area. They probably got caught in the crossfire and ended up on the Nigerian side. They are not prisoners but they live here for their own protection. It is a no-man's land. If they choose to leave, the Nigerian soldiers will wonder why they are leaving and may suspect them of being spies. The Biafrans consider them to be "soiled" by their relationship with the Nigerians and they too will probably think they're spies.

✛   ✛   ✛

As usual, I turned on my little transistor radio so I could hear the news while I ate breakfast. A selection of classical music was playing. When it ended, the commentator said, "Of course, you recognize that as the Biafran National Anthem." I shouted for Godfrey. He came running in from the small kitchen, alarmed at my unexpected cry. "Biafra!" I shouted, pointing to the radio.

He looked puzzled, smiled, and said, "Sir?"

"Biafra! It's now Biafra!"

He cried out, clapped his hands, said softly, "Biafra!"

There was wild shouting at the school block. Apparently, they had also just heard the news.

Suddenly, my large map of Nigeria taped to the living room wall came loose and fell to the ground. Both of us jumped, startled at the noise.

I whispered, "Damn!"

✛   ✛   ✛

We are situated in a side room near the entrance to the prison, probably once a prison official's office.

Outside, through the iron bars protecting the windows, we can see the refugees lined up for the food we have brought them.

Michael is finished. He keeps wiping the back of his neck with a handkerchief. We must give him something to do so he won't just stand there. He is making the patients uneasy.

I tell Inga quietly, and she sends him to the yard to help with the feeding.

Miraculously, no shells have fallen inside the prison, although they are bursting outside not too far away. I suppose the Biafrans know we are here. Maybe they're waiting for us to leave.

Owerri is one of those places that has gone back and forth, and it will probably continue to do so. I wonder if any of my former students are lobbing some of these shells. Wouldn't they be surprised to find me here! My smattering of Igbo may come in handy yet. I am thinking it could save our lives.

✛   ✛   ✛

There is another close shell. Rattle, rattle. Inga starts to say something out of the corner of her mouth, but we are interrupted by Olive walking in.

"I'm going to visit the prisoners now," she says, and tells me what to pack up for her so she can go inside. There are actual prisoners locked up in the cells underground, captured soldiers, spies, suspected spies, suspected soldiers, that sort of thing. I want to accompany her so I can look for anyone I might know, but there is no way I can leave all this to Inga. Besides, what would I do if I saw someone? It's better to stay here and assume that there is no one there I know. If I did spot a former student or fellow faculty member, how could I leave him there? What would I do? I am shuddering.

✛   ✛   ✛

The children here at the prison are especially bad off since these people have been on the run, in the rain forest, for some time. The mothers have no milk for the babies, and all of them have suffered from the elements and from exhaustion, let alone from almost nothing to eat. Everyone says he or she has lost relatives, not to the bombs and guns, but to starvation.

"I lose two childrens," says one woman, holding up three fingers. I assume the fingers are correct. She is holding a child she says is four who probably weighs 20 pounds, if that.

Styrofoam. It sits, in that all-too-familiar pose, trying to push away anyone with what little strength it has, and refusing to take any of the medicine. At least, the people here are in some sort of stable environment now, despite the shelling, and do not have to be on the run. If we can get food and medicine down this one, and all the others, then next week they should be a lot better off. No, alive and a little better off. Maybe in a few weeks' time, they'll be a lot better off.

✤ ✤ ✤

Brace takes an unaccustomed break and comes in to see how we are doing. We discuss the child I am treating at the moment. It has that look, that suspicious look of dullness that one sees so often in these kids, even in those who seem to be coming back. This one is gaining physical strength, but its mental abilities, we agree, are severely damaged. I think the mother knows, the way she hugs it to her while waiting for me to get a bottle opened.

✤ ✤ ✤

Inga says, "They've stopped," and I realize the akk-akk sounds have died out. We don't know if that's good or bad news. One thinks of how silence may mean the putting into place of a large rocket that will wipe out most of us in the prison, or whether it is the end of a small battle.

"They've started up again," I say.

We have a game which we play at the other clinics. One day we were at the Elele clinic when, all of a sudden, we saw a dozen or more army vehicles heading south, towards P.H. I speculated aloud that they were retreating and they had forgotten to tell us. Inga and Olive laughed. It became a joke: "They're heading south" is all one of us has to say if we see one or more green vehicles on the road, and the rest will have a good laugh. We don't say the obvious: If we can't joke about this situation, we can't stay in it. We do not get into the depths of our minds and our fears or we might well jump on the next truck "heading south" and never return.

"Maybe we should go south," I say to Inga, and she actually laughs out loud. One of the women turns sharply and frowns.

The shelling continues, but it sounds further away. I wonder what the range of those suckers is.

What bothers me most is that the soldiers here don't seem very confident themselves. They stand around in little cliques and smoke incessantly, gesturing, it seems, about the shelling. I suppose they are glad they are not out in the battle, although I wonder if we are worse off since we can't see over the high walls to tell if and when the shells are coming. But do I really want to be so close to see the other side actually loading a rocket-firing mechanism when that rocket could blow me apart?

✛   ✛   ✛

The people go outside the walls for water, accompanied by soldiers. How much is that accompaniment for the refugees' safety, and how much to ensure that they don't flee? But what secrets do they know?

In chess, I always hate to lose my pawns. They can be so valuable later.

✛   ✛   ✛

I have to explain to the others that the cathedral at Owerri looked like that before the war, too. It was under construction when the war began. It remains a collection of rusting girders. I must admit that it does look as if a bomb hit it.

✛   ✛   ✛

Brace comes in to tell us that he's finished. "Little noisy, huh!" he says, and I repeat the jokes about heading south. "Yep!" he says, and tells us we'll be getting about 15 more people to take care of, all adults.

I see Olive coming out of a door at the far end of the prison yard. She is accompanied by two soldiers and the three of them are smiling and chatting. The ground shakes again, and one of the soldiers says something, points to the sky, and they all laugh.

We finish the last group and Brace and Olive come to help us get packed up. The Nigerian Red Cross men have finished their food distribution, and the large lorry, also white, also dotted with red crosses back, front, sides, and top, is locked and ready to go. As soon as we load up, we climb in and wave good-bye to the soldiers running the camp.

"See you next week," I say.

Brace leads, then I come along, and then the lorry. The shelling seems to intensify as we pull out of town. I wonder if it is a coincidence.

Michael, sitting beside me, is speaking rapidly in Yoruba to two others seated beside us. He is gesturing rapidly and making rocket-exploding noises. Suddenly they all laugh, and I decide to break in.

"What a day!" I exclaim.

"My God Jehovah, what a day!" Michael says, switching to English.

"Too much!" says one of the others, and I nod my head.

"Yes," I say, slowing down for a torn-up part of the road. "Too much!"

Behind our house, as I am locking the storage door where we keep the medicines, Pius approaches. He is a little boy who has adopted our medical team. He lives with a couple of soldiers in Elele and takes care of their laundry and cooks for them. He should be the poster child of this war. His father was peacefully living in his village when the Nigerians captured it and lost it again almost immediately. When he came out of hiding after the Biafrans had regained control, the Biafran soldiers were angry that he and some other men had not joined their army, so they accused them of being spies. They shot them right in front of their families. Pius' mother, after more battles and more wins and losses, was taken captive by the Nigerians. Pius last saw her as she was screaming and struggling in the back of an army lorry headed north. The soldiers were laughing and pulling off her clothes.

He tells me this too dispassionately, then he asks me for a cigarette.

"How old are you?" I ask him.

"Fifteen."

"You are not," I say, smiling down at him.

"I'm ten years."

"You're too young to smoke." It seems ironic that I refuse him a simple cigarette when he has been through all he has been through. I imagine the soldiers give him cigarettes. He doesn't ask a second time.

✛   ✛   ✛

Olive hands me something. "A souvenir," she says. It is a small cheap spoon with a notation on the handle.

"What's 'U.B.T.H.'?" I ask.

"'University of Biafra Teaching Hospital.'"

I whistle. "Where'd you get this?"

"In Enugu." I remember she was there with some other medical people after 'liberation.' "It was incredible. They fled so fast everything was left just like it was."

"Pompeii."

"Exactly. In the main hospital they were in the middle of an operation. The instruments and everything were right there."

"What about the patient?"

She shrugs. "I don't know."

✛   ✛   ✛

Brace tells me to drive the wounded soldier to the military hospital at P.H. He has been shot up and is hooked to an I-V. One of his buddies comes along and rides in the second seat to hold the I-V in place, although it's almost impossible because the roads are so bad. If they haven't been deliberately torn up, they've been washed out by the rains. The I-V keeps coming out and I finally yell at the buddy, but then feel ashamed, as it isn't possible for anyone to keep it in. We have to stop every mile or so all the 35 miles into P.H. to replace the goddamned I-V to try to keep the man alive. He is sitting up, scrunched into one corner, and doesn't seem to know what is happening. I think we will never get to the hospital. It is like a dream where you run and run, but you never get anywhere.

✛   ✛   ✛

Every Sunday, we took two Aralen tablets to ward off malaria. It must have worked, because I got malaria the week I forgot. I sweat so much that I had to get up, pull off my soaked T-shirt, put on another, and lay a towel on the damp sheet. When I wrung out the T-shirt, I heard the sweat hit the cement floor. Two hours later, I repeated the process. Then I shivered so hard I made the metal bed squeak. I could not stop shaking.

✛   ✛   ✛

I wear my Red Cross patch on my shirt at all times. Whenever I look up and see a soldier walk into our clinic, I almost touch it to make sure he sees it. You never know if one of them has gone crazy and thinks you're a mercenary.

✛   ✛   ✛

We have another soldier brought to the house as we are about ready for bed. He has been badly wounded in an ambush somewhere to the north of us (they never say just where). His green camouflage uniform is soaked with blood. Brace cuts away the cloth and I almost get sick. His leg is mangled. He is muttering, then crying out, then murmuring in Yoruba. The men with him say he is speaking nonsense, just babbling. It strikes me that I have assumed he is speaking clearly and logically, and I realize how silly a thought that is. Brace does what he can for him and we get him calmed down somewhat. I act, if needed, as a helper at times like this.

We finally load him into a military vehicle for the ride into P.H., and I wonder if he will make it alive. I doubt it. We must have spent half an hour with him, but it seems like all night. My back hurts. They are going to drive him to the hospital right now. It must take them forever: You can't see the enormous potholes for the darkness, nor the huge dips where the culverts used to be. And the roadblocks have intensified—we wonder what is going on. We just keep ourselves informed about our clinics, and slowly move them to sites northward as the army advances (and sometimes back southward as it retreats).

✛   ✛   ✛

I say the same things over and over again, and tell them to the interpreter, who says the same things in Igbo, over and over again. "Three tablets three times a day," or "Two tablets in the morning and two tablets in the evening." The women grasp the little white paper envelopes like they are holy cards. Sometimes, I give the directions myself in Igbo, but I usually don't. I am concerned that the mothers will misunderstand me.

So often the child throws up the medicine or fights it off. The mothers, too quiet themselves sometimes, patiently wipe off the spittle from the cloth they are wearing and wait to see what I'll do next. I give the medicine all over again, after a small drink of water and a moment's respite. Usually the second time it works. If we see the mother doesn't want to force her child to take the medicine, I have the interpreter give his spiel about how the child will die unless we force it, how the child desperately needs this medicine, how this and how that until the mother seems convinced. If we cannot seem to convince them, it is their children who will be buried between now and next week's clinic.

I think of myself as an automaton sometimes, picking up bottles of pills and shaking just the right amount into the envelopes, filling bottles with just the right amount of red or green or clear liquid, saying the same phrases over and over and over again.

+ + +

I love the Harmattan season. The mornings are foggy and there is a coolness in the air you don't get the other 50 weeks of the year. If I were in a different world, it would be a good morning to have tea outside on a patio and read a crisp morning newspaper. How simple, how civilized that sounds. How utterly impossible.

+ + +

At our lunch breaks where we eat one portion of C-rations we are either effusive and almost loud, or we are quiet and spend a lot of time yawning and rubbing the backs of our necks.

+ + +

Olive is something else. She left a life of retirement in California (complete with a car with bucket seats) and charged out here to work with the other Lutherans. She has sparkling eyes and wonderfully white hair. Here we are, in the midst of a war, and she comes downstairs every morning with her make-up on, a whiff of something nice, and a smile. Then she proceeds to work her tail off during the day and into the evening, handling hundreds and hundreds of complaints, before she collapses into bed. Then, the next morning, she comes downstairs, made up, perfumed and smiling. I love it.

+ + +

For Christmas, the Red Cross in Geneva has sent us all little boxes of gifts. Included is a fine ball-point pen of a silver color with the inscription *"CICR Afrique de l'ouest Noel 1968."* That's how they get around the "Nigeria/Biafra" thing: *"Afrique de l'ouest."* How many meetings and memos did that take?

+ + +

My first Christmas Eve outside the snow and wind of the Midwest, I was getting bitten by sand flies as I sat in a Roman Catholic mass. Several of us had traveled to the ocean for a few days and we were fighting off the onslaught of thousands of tiny bugs that left red marks and itching all over the skin.

It was so odd to be so hot at midnight on December 24. We drank beer afterwards, glad to be out of the small church and away from the bugs.

+ + +

So many of those soldiers from the West and the North are wearing crucifixes, including the Tiv who are reputed to be the best fighters. I had thought they would all be Muslims. The longer I am here, the less certain I am about anything to do with this war. It seemed so set, so definite when we were at school just before and after secession. We were positive that the Nigerians who would come to fight the Biafrans would be Muslims. Good guys and bad guys. Now I am looking for the good guys. Or is it the bad guys?

+ + +

When I told someone what I did, there was a respectful, "Aaahh.... Teacher!" And, within the school, rank was carefully respected. As a university graduate, I had housing that was larger and newer than the Teacher-Training College graduates had; they, in turn, had more room than the young men with a year or so of schooling past secondary school.

At a school function, I was invited to wear my university cap and gown. When I explained I did not have them with me, there was frowning, confusion, even doubt. How could I not have brought them with me? I sensed I had insulted them, throwing, somehow, my university rank in their faces because I had taken something so difficult to achieve so lightly.

I dared not tell them that, on my graduation day, I tore off the cap and gown in the June sun and threw them on the table with the others before my parents had a chance to get a photograph. They were annoyed.

I hug Patrick, and we hold one another tightly. He has tears in his eyes. "I can't believe it," I say in a kind of stage whisper, and he shakes his head with a half-serious, half-smiling expression. His father comes out of the house.

"Teacher!" he cries. "Back in Port Harcourt!" We embrace too. The mother runs out next and Patrick reminds her in rapid English who I am. She throws up her hands to the skies and wails, then rushes at me.

I hear their stories for hours.

JANUARY 1969 – ELELE 6

Every night after dinner, Inga, Olive, and I have the four cigarettes that come with each C-ration box. Brace fusses at us, and blames me for reintroducing cigarettes into the lives of the two women. They each have one; I have two. It seems so wonderful to sit back with a cup of coffee, even if it is not very good instant Nescafe´, and light up a cigarette that is God knows how old and exhale into the night. I hope I kill at least one mosquito with every stream of smoke.

It is my one true, quiet pleasure of the day. We speak very little while we are smoking.

James and John, our two stewards, are busy making conversation while washing the dishes. It is a reminder that I must soon drive them home.

It's about half a mile to where I drop them off. There are normally two roadblocks in that distance. One is between our house and the main intersection of Elele, and the other one is around the bend, near the spot where I drop them.

Every night we approach the roadblocks at about the same time, and every night it is the same reaction from the men guarding them: screaming soldiers holding loaded guns which probably have their safeties off (if they have such devices at all), surrounded by blinding lights and more soldiers. What's worse, too often the soldiers holding those guns are drunk, so that the weapons are waving wildly about in the air.

I scream out, "Red Cross! Red Cross!" when I am challenged, but the goddamned soldiers can't hear me because they're too busy shouting for me to identify myself. One night, a few weeks ago, I got out of my Land Rover (something I have to do most nights, anyway), walked up to the man who had finally realized who I was, and said loudly, "I come through here every bloody night! At the same time, too, damnit! Why are you doing this?"

The next night, it was the same man, the same thing.

Once in a while, I will hear from the side of the road, in a voice that apparently someone thinks mimics mine, "Red Cross! Red Cross!"

The seat vibrates because James and John are shaking so hard with fear. It isn't safe for them to walk home the half mile because the soldiers are so skittish. It might mean death for the stewards, since they would suddenly appear out of the dark along the roadside and the soldiers would likely shoot first, then think about who it might be. And to go the back way, through the smattering of houses behind us to their own, could invite the same fate. Apparently, Elele is home to many deserters from other areas. And they usually have deserted with their guns—and their fears of being caught. No wonder so many people from here haven't returned. It's not safe to come back to one's own village.

Sometimes, when I have gone through the second roadblock, dropped James and John, and am on my way back, I'll be challenged *again*, so I have to suffer the soldiers two more times.

I never know what is the right thing to do. If I get down immediately and stand in front of my own headlights so they can see me, it can scare them to death. New soldiers especially think I am climbing down in order to shoot them. New and old ones shout contradictory commands ("Come down! Stay! Come down! Stay!") and I sit there, uncertain which one to obey. That's when I usually shut off my headlights and turn on the top inside light. But that can make them angry that I didn't "come down."

It is a nightly exercise that I have dubbed "come-down-advance-who-are-you-pass-through." Except that it's said a little more drunkenly, a little more excitedly, in very bad light, and much, much too often. I repeat my run-together phrase at dinner, and Olive and Brace laugh. Inga frowns and I say it slowly, then quickly again, and she too enjoys it.

I notice that there are often different soldiers and different guns. I also notice that they swing through the air in almost the same uncontrolled manner, but managing to aim at some spot on our windshield. Always.

+ + +

Every week, there were more and more roadblocks set up. A thirty-minute ride to Port Harcourt began to take more than 90 minutes. Some roadblocks were within sight of others. They seemed to be manned by civilian militia, many of whom were prostitutes and young men who had not held any regular jobs before. Some of them had guns. That frightened us.

"Come down!" they shouted at us. They examined with great detail the women's purses, invariably holding up tampons in the air and asking what they are. The women were amused at first, then angry when it continued to happen.

Whole boxes were ignored, boxes that could have contained weapons or spy materials. The roadblocks, in other words, were jokes. Jokes we wished would go away, but which, instead, proliferated.

+ + +

"If you come back quick when Nigerians liberate a place, they treat you fine-fine," says James as he slices some yam for our dinner. "They welcome me with big shouts and smiles," he continues. "*Big* shouts! And they don't forget! I see them on the road when I am walking here every morning. They greet me: 'Nigeria man!'" He giggles. "'Nigeria man!'"

"And if the Biafrans come back?" I ask.

"You eat yam in America, sir?"

"And if—?"

"I don't think they eat yam in Britain."

"No, we don't eat this kind of yam in America."

+ + +

The Biafrans attacked the hospital at Owerri, despite the huge displays of red crosses on white. Col. Henshaw told us a few weeks ago about another attack at a hospital somewhere near Enugu, but I was convinced it was propaganda, that either he made it up or someone had lied to him. Or that, if it had happened, it had been some horrible mistake. Now, I believe it. And I know it wasn't a mistake.

The hospital personnel and patients who survived have been moved down here to Elele. They are, in fact, in a former grade school across the road from us.

There are reporters from the international press in Biafra when the Nigerians bomb and strafe hospitals and refugee centers, but, unbelievably, there are no reporters here. How frustrating! This second attack, like the first, will never be known. Or, if Gowon chooses to make an announcement, the press will be likely not to believe him. Why the hell doesn't he allow the reporters and camera people in here? Or did Gowon give in to Adekunle—and his paranoia?

+ + +

P.H. is slowly coming back to life. I see my first little wooden stand by the roadside where a woman is selling cigarettes and soap. I blow my horn and wave and she flashes a smile and points rapidly to what she has for sale. I am so delighted I stop and bargain for a pack of cigarettes, probably her biggest sale of the day. At first, she thinks I want one or two from the tin on the table, but when I say I want a whole pack, she claps her hands. She dashes me a few loose matches.

And now there's a bookstore open! I buy books for all of us, musty-smelling paperbacks: Agatha Christie, a Penguin anthology of 19th-century English poetry, a couple of titles in the African Writers' Series. The others are flabbergasted when I return to the house with them, and I am interrogated as to what else there is for sale. We all spend the evening reading.

+ + +

Brace drives up a little later than expected.

"What took you so long?" Olive asks light-heartedly. We watch out for one another.

"Roadblocks," he says. "Have we got any beer? I sure could use one."

"I'll get it," I say. I catch snatches of conversation from the kitchen—"Owerri" and "worries about the Biafrans" and "I didn't get any straight answers."

It is only when I return with the big green bottle that he tells us he was shot at. Inga cries out.

"Are you OK?" I ask.

"I'm fine. It's just that they got the outside mirror. On the left."

"At least they missed the driver's side," I say.

"But," Olive says to me with a wry little smile, "aren't you glad you stayed home today, after all? That's the side you'd have been sitting on."

I look out the window at Brace's vehicle. Its white body almost glows. The red crosses shout. Brace is in his white uniform, a red-cross patch on his pocket. He was on a main road.

We are not immune.

✛　✛　✛

I aimed my camera at a modern bank building across the street from my bank in Port Harcourt. That, I thought, would make a nice slide to show people at home that there were modern buildings in Africa. Before I could snap the shutter, I saw a guard at the bank waving at me not to take the photo. I put the camera down, nodding at him, and began walking away.

The next four hours were a frightening display of near hysteria: I was taken under armed guard to the police station, interrogated by angry, shouting policemen who demanded over and over again to know what I had been doing. They did not believe that I had not taken any photos, they did not believe I was not a spy, even the bank manager did not believe I was an American.

"I lived in New York and you don't sound like an American. You sound British," he said with scorn.

I tried to explain that teaching "British English" for a year had taken away the rough edges of my American speech, but he was convinced that I was British. The former colonial masters were easy targets for frustration. For once, at least, being an American was a safer bet.

Mostly, the anger came from the fact that they didn't think I was taking "the crisis" seriously enough. And, of course, that I might have been a spy.

"Go to the villages and take photos of our mud huts," one man said.

I tried to explain that I had done that but that I wanted Americans to see the modern buildings as well. The man knew we had modern buildings in America. He said he knew we did not have mud huts. Why would I want such a photo? Suspicion reigned.

Finally, after several levels of policemen had all vented their anger at me, I was ushered into the top man's office. He beckoned me to sit down, offered me a cigarette and told me, with the hint of a smile, that I was a "foolish boy" and I should have known better than to carry a camera around with the "war hysteria" in the air.

The next week, he allowed me to retrieve my camera, film intact.

Col. Henshaw stops by for a beer. He comes by every couple of weeks and has a drink and shares his cigarettes and gossip. There is a female army officer called "The Matron" who sometimes accompanies him now. She works at the hospital across the road. The Matron keeps her hair in many, tight braids under her cap and doesn't let Henshaw get ahead of her in numbers of glasses of beer consumed or numbers of cigarettes smoked. She is loud and brassy with a sense of humor that tries to make you think she does not realize she is funny. She says something, we and Henshaw laugh, and she pretends surprise.

There is much talk of what will happen "after the war." A soldier who comes for Henshaw tells me I must come visit him in the North "after this war be finish" and he will give me one of his sisters. I feel like I'm in an old Bob Hope "Road" picture.

We are walking along the main road in Elele for a Sunday afternoon stroll when Henshaw comes out of his headquarters and calls for us to come join him in a drink. The idea of a cold beer has us accepting his offer immediately. Even if it didn't sound good, we would be hesitant to refuse his offer of hospitality. We must stay on good terms with the officers so we are allowed into the new villages as they secure them and to remain in the ones we are already serving. Whenever I find it uncomfortable to socialize with one of the soldiers, I have to remind myself that they could easily make it impossible for us to go into the villages to work.

One of the roadblocks, the first one I come to at night, is a few yards south of the veranda on which we are enjoying our beers. In the daytime, the soldiers are calm; they mill about, laughing with one another. Their guns are resting at the side of the crude barrier they have erected. The men are sober.

Suddenly, for some reason, a civilian starts to walk around the roadblock instead of stopping to answer questions. Henshaw and I are facing that way. He shouts at the soldiers to grab the man. They drag him to the house. The man is stiff. Henshaw goes from his well-modulated English to Pidgin and begins haranguing the man, asking him what he has been doing, and why. The man is terrified. We sit there in silence. Henshaw pulls his gun from its holster and brandishes it in front of the man's face. "I tink I go kill-am," he says. Olive looks very pale. I am looking down at the man's feet. His whole body is shaking. I do not think that Henshaw will shoot him, or even physically harm him, but I am not sure when to intervene or what to say other than the obvious, "Don't shoot him, please."

Henshaw puts his gun away and orders the man to go on his way. Apparently, the man, who has recently come to Elele from the bush, didn't think it was necessary to go through the roadblock in the daytime. He stutters loudly to the soldier who escorts him off the veranda that he thought it was for vehicles only.

The conversation is difficult to get going again. Fortunately, our beers are almost gone, so we finish them and make our good-byes. One of the characteristics of this living situation that I find most unusual is that we often do not discuss such a thing after it has passed. We find, I guess, that we cannot dwell on the war, although we hardly ignore it as a topic. In a case like Henshaw and the gun, we have our own emotions and reactions right there and then. It isn't something we need—or want—to discuss all over again immediately afterwards. I don't mention it to Brace, and I don't know if the women do or not. Probably not.

On top of all that these children are going through, there is now a measles epidemic sweeping the area. And something like this knows no borders, so it is probably in Biafra now, too. Because of the larger numbers of children who are critically ill, the deaths from measles in Biafra are probably even more than here.

We prepare to give them fluids. The nurses stick tubes into their stomachs. Teams of medical and paramedical people are arriving to "shoot" the population with injection "guns." We try, in the hearing of the soldiers, not to call them that for fear we will arouse suspicions.

There is a small boy at Elele Alimini named Thankgod. He is just now recovering from *kwashiorkor*. And suddenly he has the measles. He looks up at me, and through me, and the vital clear fluids drip, drip, drip into his body. What endurance the kids who survive must have. We look over the makeshift clinic filled with cots and pads of little ones attached to the bottles. Olive looks very old and very tired today. We do something unusual, the two of us: we stop on the way back and take a walk along the creek west of Elele. I begin to throw stones into the water while she sits on a big rock. I throw the stones and throw the stones harder and harder.

We don't have a guard outside our house anymore. The first month we had one faithfully. He almost kept us awake with his snoring. We lock all the doors and the windows and hope for the best. This house could be taken in a minute if anyone wanted it. A band of crazy deserters or Biafrans or regular Nigerian soldiers could come up here and, for whatever reason, bump us all off. The locking of the doors and windows is really to keep the unarmed thieves out. They are the known devils.

An American named Arthur who has been sent out by the ICRC in Lagos to help with the measles campaign is staying in our house. He has recently come to Nigeria.

Today, I am taking him from Elele to Ahoada so he can "shoot" the children there. We have just stopped to leave some supplies with the others who are handling the crowds at Elele.

On the road once again, Arthur says, with fervor, "What a terrible thing this is here!"

"What thing?" I am genuinely confused.

"Why, this war, the diseases, the children. You know." He seems puzzled.

"I'm supposed to pick you up at 4 o'clock this afternoon," I say. I chew on a toothpick.

"You mean you're not staying with me?"

"No, Brace needs me back at the clinic. You'll have a couple of guys there to help you. They're our interpreters at Ahoada. Nice chaps." I say it as clipped as I can, in my best British way. I am impatient. I want to get back to the clinic.

"Let me say something." He turns in his seat to face me.

"Shoot. It's a free country. Well, actually, it's not, that's just an expression I brought over— "

"None of you seems to be particularly *upset* about what's going on here. Don't you think," he says, "it's a horrible thing, what's happening here? Look around you, children dying, soldiers dying, fighting all over the place, starvation—"

"—all over the place."

"Yes. All over the place."

"I still put my pants on one leg at a time." That just comes out.

"What—?"

"I mean that, whatever is going on here, I still go on. You just do, that's all."

"But, don't you ever want to—"

"Look," I say, "there are your interpreters now. The one on the left is Opoku and the one on the right is Jesse. They're brothers. You'll like them."

When Brace offers to pick up Arthur at four o'clock, I do not give the expected protest. I spend the time packing the boxes of supplies we have had at the clinic today. There are fewer syringes to dispose of than usual. I am not sure if that is good news or bad news.

✛   ✛   ✛

I am heading towards the Umu Nelu clinic with a couple of the Nigerian Red Cross men when I see a big army lorry filled with soldiers coming our way. We always pull off the road if we need to, as they simply demand that everything else get out of the way. I start to pull off to the left when I realize the grinning driver is playing a deadly game: I have to get completely out of the way or we will have a head-on accident and our little Land Rover, no matter how sturdy it is, will lose against the big Mercedes lorry. I smash us into a big log. The front left fender crumples.

+ + +

Olive's face is pink with anger. "Get those boxes off this table!" she shouts at me.

I am startled, and jump to obey her. "Don't you ever do that again! We can't operate this clinic that way!" She slams down her black medical bag on the spot I have just cleared.

"I need this space," she continues. "You know that! Put the boxes over there where they belong."

A half-dozen old women are surrounding her, pulling at her sleeves, slapping one hand into the other in the sign of begging. "Give me, give me," they say, and point to the medicines.

Olive's eyes snap. "Get out!" she shouts at them. "Get out!"

Then she turns to me once again. "Don't just stand there! Get the rest of your stuff unloaded!" She storms out and is lost almost immediately in a sea of people crowding around her, crying out for medicines. She does not respond, but looks for the weakest children, then hands cards to their mothers and points them towards the room where Brace is already busy with other children. I watch her, amazed how calm she can be, then have to laugh to myself when, in the midst of my admiration, an old woman pulls on her sleeve one too many times and Olive turns to her and says something sharp I cannot hear, but can imagine. She then moves on immediately to touch a child, rub its face soothingly, and hand a card to its mother.

There is no way I can explain to her, and certainly not now, how I feel about her shouting at me in front of the Nigerians. I dare not say to her what I would like: "Bravo!" Too many whites in the tropics have long felt one should not disagree with other whites in the presence of "the natives."

I find her attitude refreshing. But if I dare tell her, she will probably hit me with a large bottle of something and maybe ask questions later. Maybe.

✛ ✛ ✛

Americans from Oklahoma, Texas and Louisiana lived in abundance in Port Harcourt. Their accents were difficult for us to understand, sometimes, and the Nigerians were often completely at a loss. They were the "oil people." Most of the men had previously worked for Shell Oil in a variety of jobs in Venezuela and the U.S. The women, who seemed either to be raw and big-boned or incredibly tiny and pale, visited one another's homes to play cards, drink, complain about their servants and about the country as a whole. They went to the club where they swam, as well as played cards, drank, and complained about their servants or the country as a whole.

Only now and then did they give Nigerians a compliment. "The colored here are different than at home," one would say and the others would nod, then pour everyone another round of drinks.

✛ ✛ ✛

The sand flies are about to drive us all mad. Every dawn and dusk they arrive, and our mosquito nets are useless. The holes could not be made small enough to keep the sand flies out and let any air in. Having one's body covered with a rash of bites is preferable, I guess, to suffocating to death, rashless. I am given a large canister of insecticide, which I pump and spray all around the house. It gives temporary relief.

✛ ✛ ✛

We do the rare thing of going to a party in P.H. The three of us drive in after we get home, with promises to ourselves to fill the trays in time for the next clinic. We try to talk Brace into coming in, too, but he doesn't want to. I think he feels guilty about going to a party; so do we, but we three agree it sounds too inviting. And we need it.

The get-together takes place on a large lawn behind the mess hall. There are lanterns strung about, and lots and lots of booze and little kebabs of fried meat which we discreetly avoid. We're not sure they are diarrhea-proof. The crowd is mostly military men and prostitutes. The women are dolled up in enormous wigs and long dresses. Some are beautiful. Some merely have that look of Nigerian prostitutes: too much make-up, too much bosom, too many teeth flashing in their smiles. A band plays High Life and I dance often. One of the men compliments me on my dancing and I thank him. When he asks me where I have learned how to dance High Life, I say, "Port Harcourt." I don't think he'd ever understand if I told him I learned in Peace Corps training. In Atlanta, Georgia.

Adekunle weaves back and forth and holds onto a chair for support. He makes a drunken speech about Black Power and white racism, white guilt, white this and white that. After he helps himself slowly down off the porch, he sits down at a nearby table of whites. I can hear them laughing all the way over at our table. Adekunle laughs the loudest.

Later, he stops the band a second time, and speaks to us again. He is angry because he disagrees with something *Time* said about the war. He lights the issue with his cigarette lighter and the crowd cheers.

"Oh, hell," I whisper to Olive, "if he's going to burn every magazine he disagrees with, we'll be here all night."

He throws the magazine into the air, and the flames cast a glow on his dark glasses. "*Time* magazine!" he shouts at the smoldering remains on the lawn in front of him. "Ha! The Black Scorpion makes you black too!" The crowd cheers again.

We are eventually summoned to meet him. He is one of those people who looks just like his photos. Intense. Evil. I stand in line behind the Red Cross women and with Dr. Martin. Only Inga and I have never met him before. Dr. Martin introduces me. Adekunle shakes my hand stiffly. He has chatted briefly with the women, who all flashed him smiles, but with me he merely nods and gives a hint of a smile. He frightens me. He frightens the women, too, perhaps even more than me, but none of us shows it, I don't think. We are immediately ushered off the little stage and back to our tables.

I hear him laughing again.

+ + +

The P.H. team has toilet paper that says on the wrapper, "Made in Biafra." That will probably be a collector's item someday, but we just tear it off and throw it away. I still have hope for Biafra; perhaps that's why I don't save things like that. If there will always be a Biafra, it really won't be a collector's item. I have managed to get a few stamps and bank notes and those I will save. Just for souvenirs. Or reminiscence pieces, I guess. I just hope the military doesn't search our house someday for whatever reason and find my little cache. Some of the soldiers would jump to such horrible conclusions.

+ + +

Some of the mothers laugh at my Igbo and even pat my arm in appreciation. Others turn quizzically to the interpreters because they don't believe what they are hearing. When it is confirmed, they too laugh or smile down at their children.

The children never even look up.

+ + +

What would happen, I wonder, if I sent an anonymous letter to General Gowon telling him he should allow the foreign press in here to find out the truth on this side of the front lines....As quickly as I think it, I dismiss it. Not that it isn't a good idea; it's just that a head of state is not going to read such a letter. Some lackey would keep it to himself. And, besides, we hand our mail to the P.H. team to hand it to the Cessna pilot headed for Lagos. A name and address like that would not go unquestioned.

+ + +

Patrick tells me how they locked all their doors and windows and hid, listening to the gunfire and shelling. They stayed inside for hours, then for days, afraid to go outside, afraid to open any door or window to peek outside, hoping the soldiers from both sides would think the building were abandoned. It worked. No one bothered them. They waited and waited. Finally, there was quiet. They cautiously opened a window to peer outside. Nothing.

They opened a door and walked outside. No one else was on the street.

Only later did they find others who had done the same thing. The soldiers believed them.

"We were safe," Patrick said. His little brother laughed, remembering it all over again, too. "We were safe," he said, as if Patrick had not just said it.

"Teacher," their mother said, coming into the room with a bottle and a glass on a tray. "Beer." Old times. Cold beer. Laughter. We were safe.

✛ ✛ ✛

At my school, there is dried human feces on the floor of my former living room. Broken glass is strewn along one wall as if someone were drunk and kept dropping bottle after bottle. Nonsense stuff written in English is across part of a wall. All the furniture, of course, is gone. I'm surprised the toilet stool is still there.

And the geckos. We have no figures on how many of those little lizards were killed so far in this war, but I'll bet it wasn't more than half a dozen. They rush away from any disturbance, unlike the people who get trapped by bombs and ambushes and rapidly changing front lines. The two geckos on the living-room wall dart about in that silly fashion of theirs, looking for insects. I wave my hand at them and they scurry away. In my preoccupation with them, I almost step in some shit right where my dining table used to be.

The side of the house is smeared with machine-gun holes. That *was* a bomb that was dropped on the main building. And everything is gone. Not one room anywhere on the campus has anything in it. Even the tabernacle in the chapel has been roughly pried open.

All the books I classified and catalogued and checked out to eager kids! I find one book in the front of the main building, opened face down in the wild grass, rotting rapidly.

What an incredible waste. That book cannot match the child who sits listless, scabied and bloated, but it is still a waste, still a tragedy of its own kind.

One thing can be said for books: They can be replaced.

There is, unfortunately, no newly opened store in Port Harcourt selling children, even slightly musty ones, children who come with smiles, children who can run and yell.

✛　✛　✛

I was reading one of the books from the Peace Corps book locker when I felt a sharp sting on one of my big toes. A large bug had bitten me. I slapped it to death with my sandal, and brushed it out of the way. Minutes later, I put down my book in time to see a long row of ants, trailing in through an open window several feet away, carrying the dead bug out of the house. Although I found the whole affair somewhat creepy, I watched in fascination. They got the bug up the wall and were having trouble lifting him up over the windowsill (the bug was several times their size) until I gently pushed him over the obstacle. "Good luck," I said. I denied to myself that I had been friendly to them so they wouldn't come back for me.

✛　✛　✛

"I have no money," says one of our interpreters when we are having a discussion of the war. Two or three others say the same thing. There is no cash here. The soldiers bring some with them but they mostly barter—trading cigarettes or things they've looted—or they go ahead and take what they like.

And the civilians, if they have anything at all, have Biafran currency or that old Nigerian stuff that was pulled out of circulation when these people were inside Biafra. Even showing either of those to anyone can get them into a lot of trouble.

We do pay our two stewards in cash. They are probably the wealthiest civilians in Elele right now. Money! I have thought of this war in terms of the loss of lives and time and potential, but I haven't really given much thought to the loss of money.

The interpreter's comment startles me. I can empathize with only a little money, but *no* money? It's a concept I can't come to grips with. I'm sure our interpreter can't either.

✛　✛　✛

We must pack quickly for a possible evacuation. The Biafrans are on their way south, rapidly it seems, although we can't get much information. We worry about the clinics near and in Owerri. Is all that work now in vain? James, our steward, is utterly despondent. He dares not stay in Elele. If he does, and the Biafrans arrive, he will be declared a collaborator, although his "crime" is wanting to lead a normal, safe life.

I stuff what money I have into a bag, along with a minimum of personal belongings. Everything else is pushed into the cheap *armoire* with the intention of abandoning it. I am reminded of my evacuation from school at the beginning of this same war. I left so much behind and traveled with the clothing on my back for a very long time.

I am tired of evacuations.

+ + +

"They took branches and scratched the outsides of the houses. The noise excited the goats, and that's how they found them."

"Did they eat them?"

"Of course." My former student—alive!—looks at me as if he thinks I am stupid. What else do you do with goats? These men were not farmers, after all, but Nigerian soldiers on the move.

"They killed and cooked them. What a feast!"

"Why didn't you take them with you when you fled?"

"Too much noise. Goats make noise all the time. And if they were in the bush, the Nigerians know we too are in the bush. Too dangerous!"

I am sympathetic, but my feelings are tempered by memories of eating goat at a wedding once.

"Do you eat goat in America?"

I have been asked this before. I don't know why. No one ever asks if we eat chicken or fish. "Not too much," I say, wondering if I know anyone in all of America who has ever tasted goat.

"They took the branches and *scraped* them along the sides of our houses!" He makes a mock swoop. "Soldiers!"

Soldiers.

FEBRUARY 1969 – ELELE

I slam right through a roadblock.

"Duck!" I yell to Anthony, the Nigerian Red Cross worker sitting beside me. He ducks. And he swears. I swear too.

It happens at that otherwise peaceful roadblock on the way back from Elele Alimini, right on this side of town. The soldier comes up and demands medicine. Sometimes Brace will give them something if they really seem sick, but I refuse to second-guess a complaint in Pidgin English. That makes him angry. He demands that I open my door and get down. I shake my head no. With a vigor. Then he demands that I give him a ride to Elele and I refuse. He gets even angrier. Luckily, he isn't holding a gun, or I don't imagine I would be so bold. I can't smell anything, but I think he's drunk. Or high on something, more likely. I shift into first gear very slowly and turn to Anthony.

"Get ready," I whisper and nod ever so slightly down the road ahead. He gets hold of the seat.

The soldier, now furious, goes around to the back of the vehicle and is about to climb inside when I take off. The long heavy stick across the road flies up against us and I am afraid it is going to break the windshield, but it sails up over us instead, landing hard on top of our roof. That noise scares me—for a second I think it is some kind of missile from the man at the roadblock.

In my outside mirror, I see the soldier shaking his fist in the air.

We keep saying to one another, "Duck! Duck!" and laughing. It helps relieve our tension. I was worried, I tell Anthony, that the man might have demanded the vehicle or started helping himself to all the medicines we have in the back, some of which are lethal if not used properly. All those syringes we always break up at night certainly would come in handy if he wanted to sell the medicines later. Why, just wash them out in river water, hang up a sign, and you're in business.

I am thinking he might show up at the house later tonight. Hide the big red cross on the front!

+ + +

When we arrive back at the house, I pull around behind as I always do, so we can unload the supplies and fill up the two Land Rovers with petrol. (I have to suck on the hose coming from the big 50-gallon drums until the petrol begins to flow— sometimes right in my mouth if I'm not quick enough. I am often, very often, not quick enough.) Right there, right in front of where we are going to unload, is a soldier standing with a huge pile of rifles. For a second I connect his presence with what I have just done at the roadblock and I think they have come for me, in force.

I slam on the brakes, and Anthony is thrown against the dash. "Damn!" I yell.

The soldier smiles at me and actually salutes, and my fears of any instant retribution for tearing through the roadblock evaporate. He comes over to my window. "Good evening, sah!" he says with a smile.

I smile back weakly. "What are those?" I ask, pointing to the rifles. There must be 50 of them.

"From deserters, sah. We take-m today from here." He waves his hand across the back of the village.

I turn to Anthony. "A raid." He nods.

"Why are they here?" I ask the soldier. He seems slightly puzzled by that question.

"Oh, this be good place, sah." Just then the others arrive from Umu Nelu. Brace jumps down immediately.

"What the hell is this?" he asks all of us.

"They made a raid today on the deserters in Elele," I say.

He turns to the soldier. "Get that damned stuff out of here," he says. He is shaking. "We are the Red Cross, not some sort of ammunition dump."

The soldier seems puzzled again. He must have thought we would reward him for his good sense to bring the rifles here. He calls to a couple of others standing on the veranda near the guns, and tells them that they must take the guns away from the Red Cross people. They begin to remove them.

✛ ✛ ✛

I share my news of the roadblock running with Brace, prepared for his wrath, but he doesn't seem angry. In fact, he says it is what I should have done, and he doesn't think anything is going to happen. Nevertheless, I wait for a lorry to roar up our long driveway to take me away. Now my only fear is that the soldier at the roadblock will be waiting for me when I return to Elele Alimini. Maybe he was so high he won't remember at all what he did. Maybe he won't recognize my face. Maybe.

✛ ✛ ✛

Suddenly there are terrible screams outside; the people are running for the bush behind the schoolhouse. Roaring into the school compound come half a dozen army vehicles. In seconds, there isn't a person left except us and the interpreters, who must feel some safety being around us. Inside one of the lorries is an army man who was shot only minutes ago somewhere north of here. A whole contingent has brought him for Brace to look at. He spends some minutes with the wounded man. Inga helps translate from Hausa. Brace patches up a nasty looking wound and gives his buddies instructions to take him on into P.H. to the military hospital.

The soldiers pull out again and the people return, slowly, then quickly, and with a lot of nervous laughter. No one knew when the soldiers first pulled in which side they were on. Either one could mean danger. It is incredible what little regard so many of the soldiers have for the civilians. They must find it funny in a terribly perverse way to charge into hundreds of people like that and watch them scream and head for cover. It is so cruel. These people have been through too much to have to put up with the shenanigans of a bunch of cowboys.

✦ ✦ ✦

Three or four of the Nigerian Red Cross men and I go to Umuagu every Thursday to take food. "These people," says one of the soldiers there. "They are Nigerians by day and Biafrans by night." He laughs, shakes his head, and keeps his eyes on the line of people forming to receive food.

"We take them to the fields to work every day, you know," he says to me. I don't know. I shake my head. "Oh, yes, we take them there with these." He pats his gun. "Listen, these people are Ibos, man, and they need protection from the Biafrans." He spits out the word. "You think all Ibos unite. Think one more time, man."

In effect, we are feeding these soldiers. I recognize many women in our line who are the prostitutes who are living with them. They collect enough food for themselves, their children, and the men. Compared to them, the village women look so plain, so small, so simple. I catch one young village woman looking at a prostitute. She touches her own hair and smoothes down her frayed blouse. Then she sees me watching her. A quiet, "Oh!" and then she puts her hand to her mouth to try to hide her smile. I don't hide mine. I touch my hair, mimicking her, then run my hand down my shirt and, across sacks of dried fish, we both laugh.

✦ ✦ ✦

We have a new interpreter today. When we are alone, he explains what happened. "Jonathan has gone," he tells me.

"Gone where?" I can't imagine going anywhere.

"He went for bush," he whispers. He looks around. "Biafra."

"Why? For—"

"He fears Biafrans too much. He is afraid they catch him here and call him 'collaborator.'"

"But you aren't—" One of the Nigerian soldiers comes in.

"Give me aspirin tablet," he says.

"I don't have medicines," I say. The interpreter continues sacking up the powdered milk.

"You Red Cross," the soldier says. He frowns. The interpreter stops sacking and keeps his head down.

"Me na Red Cross *food* man," I reply. "No be Red Cross *medicine* man. He dey Port Hakkut."

"Eeee!" The soldier says, his lament echoing in the small room. He snaps his fingers. "Eeee! Make somebody dey give me aspirin tablet!" He walks out and we hear him say one more "Eeee!"

✤ ✤ ✤

We had a first-aid kit given to us by the Peace Corps doctor. There was a bottle of something to use if you were bitten by a snake. I picked it up to read the instructions, hoping against hope that this was merely a precautionary exercise. Sometimes, when I was lying in bed, I imagined how many snakes were within a square mile of my bedroom, and I had to start thinking of something else. "Square mile?" my mind taunted. "How about thinking in square feet?" I was always afraid I would dream of snakes slithering into my bedroom, sliding up the metal legs of the bed and coming at me under the mosquito netting, but, fortunately, I was spared such horrors.

✤ ✤ ✤

The old man stands at the window of my Land Rover. He speaks to me, but I think he is saying it for the benefit of the soldiers, who seem not to be listening. "My fadda know no Biafra. His fadda know no Biafra. Why, man, muss I know Biafra?" He holds up his hands. "What be dis ting call Biafra?"

✤ ✤ ✤

Our young friend Pius has surfaced after being gone for a few weeks. Apparently he made a trek to his village and found no one back there yet, so he returned and has moved back in with his soldiers. He and I sit outside in the dark on the front steps and talk about the war. He is the one person I know who seems incapable of talking about anything else. He asks so many questions about it; most of them begin with "why." And almost none of them can I answer to his satisfaction.

Then he begins asking about America. He asks me if we have black people there. Will I take him to live with me there. Can I get him into a school. How much are the school fees. Will I buy him some shoes. Will I help him look for his mother. Are there any Muslims in America. He wants to know what we eat, what we wear to school, do we have wars like this one.

As I sit there looking into the house, where everything is dark and there is no noise, I ponder his one question: "Do you have wars like this in America?"

I bitterly answer, "No, we export ours. It's safer." He doesn't understand, of course, so I explain just a bit about Vietnam and he goes on to other questions. His concern is whether or not it would be safe in America, or would he have to worry about being shot or taken away.

How many Americans my age are sitting right now, in the dark and in the almost quiet of that dark, looking through the tropical vegetation of Vietnam. Or maybe it's already light there. I am not in the mood to figure out time zones. How many Americans are cradling rifles, or holding onto dead babies. Or flying airplanes over the rain forests dropping bombs on little Piuses? How removed those pilots must feel as they fly along, pushing and pulling little levers to release their bombs that go dropping onto villages far below. How very removed.

I have been sent some information by a friend about going to Canada or Sweden. I can't go to Vietnam to create more Piuses or kill the Piuses themselves. Not after this. War: that last great horror we inflict upon ourselves.

"When you go home, are you going to fight in Vietnam?"

I shake my head violently, forgetting that he cannot see me in the dark.

"Sir?" he asks.

"No," I whisper. "No."

✛   ✛   ✛

I stop to take some pictures in a village on my way back from P.H. I don't even know its name. We must be so careful not to take photos where the military can see us, but this time I feel it will be safe. I pull off the road a few hundred yards and walk a little way amidst the empty compounds.

Here and there in the greenery of the palm trees, the banana trees, the vines and the grass, there are flowers. Those pretty pink ones with the large blossoms, so delicate and quiet, standing at the end of the compound, waiting patiently for me to take their photos. "War?" they say to me. "Is there a war?"

The roofs are missing from most of the buildings, the thatch not having survived the rains since the people fled. Even some of the walls of the mud houses are now disintegrating because the roofs are not there to protect them.

It is eerie, more eerie than a ghost town I once saw in our own West because here, at least, you know that people have been present only months ago; you can almost hear the soldiers from Biafra haranguing the people to be brave, for the men to join the army, for the women and children to support them against the "vandals." Then the battle, the flight, the entry of the Nigerians, the looting.

I sit on the ground right in the middle of a compound and take a photo of a house at the far end. Here, in the compound, the women have done their cooking and the children have played and the men have come home from whatever they had to come home from, and I can imagine the smells of the early evening when gentle conversations and laughter could be heard across the village, when one could see the glow of the red coals under the cooking pots. And the inevitable lusty cries of healthy babies.

And now there is only a crazy white man sitting on his butt in the middle of this same compound taking a picture of what is left. Some people have returned to most of the other villages, but this one is still vacant. I have watched for signs of life whenever I pass this way each time I go and come from P.H., but it is always empty. It is possible that everyone is dead. It isn't that big a village and maybe everyone "went for bush" and died of starvation and disease and occasional gunfire. What happens then? When this bloody war finally ends, what happens to this village? Already the rain forest is reclaiming it. Some of the houses on the edge of the village have vines growing over them. The heavy rains are helping make the mud houses only mud once again.

Ashes to ashes, dust to dust.

✢ ✢ ✢

Sometimes, when I was visiting a student in his village, I tried to peer out the window into the compound before I emerged to cries of "Good morning!" and the rush of little children coming at me to shake my hand and rub the hair on my arms. If I was lucky, there were boards with cracks big enough so that I could secretly watch the early-morning activity. The women wrapped layers of cloth around themselves, securing their babies to their backs. Other women came into the compound with heavy loads of firewood balanced on their heads. The children were everywhere, running and laughing, like children anywhere. Older children were sent on errands and given chores. The men, their wrappahs secured around their waists, emerged from doorways, chewing sticks in their mouths, combs in their hands. It was so Norman Rockwell, I thought, and laughed at how hard it would have been to convince the arriving American overwhelmed by the seeming strangeness of it all.

The Red Cross sends us still more reports. In one week last month, all of us fed 660,000 and gave medical attention to 34,000. I swear there are some days when it feels like that many were seen just by our team.

Olive is walking this way with an armful of mail. Yes! Yes! It has been at least a month since we got any.

Brace is listening to Radio Biafra just to see what they are saying there. An air of hysteria dominates all the Radio Biafra broadcasts. And the sarcasm drips off the lips of the commentators.

The Biafran National Anthem is just coming on. I smile. Wasn't that 20 years ago? Weren't the roads in reasonable shape and the children laughing?

Two more students. They are at Patrick's house when I stop to see him before heading back to Elele with the new supplies.

"When the Biafrans were leaving Oron, they rounded us all up," said Gerald, the one who used to sweep the library and reshelve the books.

"Yes," cuts in Josiah. "They told us to meet them at one of the petrol stations, down near the big market."

"Shell-BP," says Gerald.

"Yes, Shell-BP," says Jonathan.

Gerald is smoking, puffing quickly on the small menthol cigarette Patrick's father has given him.

"We were going there," he continues, "but we got suspicious. So we ran for bush. They began shooting at us."

"What did they want?" I think I know.

"They wanted us to flee with them. All of us were schoolboys. No village boys."

"We ran!" says Jonathan. He slaps his hand on his knee. "They shouted and they shot their guns, but we ran."

Gerald is more solemn. "When the Nigerians came the next morning, we went to the village. The old men went first. Then they signaled for us to come."

Jonathan picks some loose tobacco from his teeth.

"Biafra!"

MARCH 1969 – ELELE

Once again, I feel so very white.

I have not felt quite so apart since that day when I was walking across our school compound with my fellow teachers, that must have been two years ago by now, and some of my students were kicking a soccer ball round. The other teachers and I joined them for an impromptu keep-away sort of game. Suddenly, one of the teachers didn't know where to kick it to keep it from the students, and Amadi, my next-door neighbor and drinking buddy, said, *"Onye ocha!* To the *onye ocha!"*

I was crushed. Was I just a "white man" to him? Couldn't he have used my name? I wouldn't have been so surprised had it been my first week there, or if it had been his first week there, but we had been friends for almost a year, going places together and sitting down at one another's table for coffee or beer or for one of our Tuesday-morning palm wine sessions. Thinking back, I say, "Hmmph," out loud. I seem to dredge up the past quite a bit these days, probably because I leave here in a couple of weeks and I have no idea when I'll be back to Nigeria or anywhere else in Africa.

✛   ✛   ✛

I am looking earnestly for something at the Ahoada market to take back home—a small gift—when a bunch of women set up a cry: "White man! *Onye ocha!* White man!" Others gather around and clap their hands and smile. Some begin singing a little ditty which has "*onye ocha*" in it.

"*Onye ogi!*" I shout at them, and they scream with delight. The fact that I can reply in Igbo, and call them *their* color, astounds them and amuses them. But, instead of calming them down, it excites them and makes it impossible for me to shop. I planned to spend an extra, valuable 15 minutes or so in the market before going back to Elele but, instead, I decide to drive off. I can hear them shouting at me for hundreds of yards. I pull off the road as soon as I round the corner. I rub my eyes, then blow air out of my mouth, full blasts of hot air. I need to go.

✤ ✤ ✤

Three years ago this month I was a college senior with a letter telling me I had been selected to train to be a Peace Corps teacher in Nigeria. I knew just about where it was, and I remember there had been a *coup d'etat* a short time before. End of knowledge. Now, in a minute way, I am helping Nigeria make its history.

Rueful laughs and sighs. I curse, punctuating my own silence.

✤ ✤ ✤

I want to believe that Biafra will survive. I want it to be worthwhile. I want all the death and destruction to have meant something. If it falls and does not rise again, what terrible, terrible sacrifices will have been made. For nothing.

✤ ✤ ✤

Olive, Inga and I play gin rummy. Brace has gone to bed with a cold. Olive wins. She has the bluest eyes that absolutely glow when she lays her hand down on the table and says triumphantly, "Gin!" She says it a few too many times for Inga and me ever to catch up.

I was going to try to make a Monopoly game out of cardboard from the boxes we get medicines in, but I couldn't remember all the names and didn't want to do anything but the original. It was going to be a surprise for Inga's birthday, which turned out to be last week. We got suspicious. She suddenly got a lot of cards in the last batch of mail.

Instead of Monopoly, I drew her a funny picture and wrote some of the "dirty" Danish words on it (with my own guesses as to their spelling). She had to say the words slowly aloud to try to make them out, as she first thought they were English. When she caught on, she had a very good laugh. Much better than Boardwalk and Park Place

✣　✣　✣

Olive rolls in from Port Harcourt about 9 p.m., long after dark, and is greeted by the three of us who have stayed up reading. Not one of us admitted that we were worried about her, but I noticed that the other two, like me, looked up every time we heard a vehicle on the road. We all go to bed almost immediately.

✣　✣　✣

It is my turn to read the scripture this morning. There are little books belonging to the Lutherans that we read from at morning and evening meals. Then there is a prayer offered. The first time it was my turn for the prayer, we bowed in silence. I cannot bear to pray aloud. I cannot reconcile God and those children we face every day. Someone needs to tell God to wave His magic wand.

Olive last night began to read the scripture, "Suffer the little children to come unto me...." She managed to get that far, and then she sat there and clenched her jaw and rocked back and forth. She exited for a few minutes. Inga wiped tears away from her eyes. I stared into my soup. Brace was silent.

✣　✣　✣

We are driving over to Ahoada to visit Col. Muhammed. He stopped by this afternoon to invite us to visit him at his new headquarters, and the women and I are going. Brace does not like to do these things, and, as long as we make an appearance, it doesn't matter if he goes or not. We will make an excuse for him— he's tired, he's seeing a patient, he's writing out reports for Lagos on the numbers of people we're treating. Something like that.

Here is Elele Alimini and here is the place where I so bravely/ foolishly ran through the roadblock. I have never seen that soldier again. Anthony and I have that as our little joke: "Duck!" is like a password with us, and it gets us and the other Nigerian Red Cross men to laughing whenever one of us calls it out.

We see someone walking along the road now and then; it is really getting populated in this area again. Old men stop and turn to see us come upon them, and they raise their hands in a slow greeting. They walk with long, knobby sticks. I am reminded of the films I have seen of the old Chinese men in their long clothes, and their very long faces, with intent eyes that look into you and your headlights as your approach them. They make the pretense of waving you along.

Col. Muhammed is waiting for us. He sends immediately for some beer. Muhammed asks the women many questions about themselves. Once in a while he throws a question my way. I am used to this. He is delighted to find that Inga works in the North. It is not his area, but the North is "the best part of Nigeria."

"And you," he says to me. "Man, what will you do when you leave here?"

"I'm going to travel," I say.

"To the North?" I answer that, yes, I will visit the North.

"Good, good," he says, suddenly seeming more interested in me. "Visit Kano. Kaduna. Maiduguri. Beautiful places."

"Yes," I say. I'm not sure at all if I'll get to any of them.

He turns to the women once again, satisfied that I am all right, that I will go to the North and visit his beautiful places. My beer is warming up just enough that I can sip some of it. I am afraid that if I drink it too fast, I'll be given another big bottle to drink. Each of us has been handed a big Star beer bottle and I know Inga won't be able to drink half of hers; Olive, on the other hand, may surprise me and get hers all down. If I drink even this one, I'm not sure how steady a hand I'll have for the drive back. To say nothing of handling the godawful roadblocks.

✛   ✛   ✛

The ground shakes violently. There is a terrible sound immediately outside the front door. The three of us jump up. Inga screams. There is a lot of shouting outside.

Muhammed laughs and goes to the door. He opens it and points. "Anti-aircraft gun! It's wonderful!" He laughs again. "You really got frightened, didn't you?" He looks at me. "And you, you are supposed to be brave, you're a man. But you jumped like the others!" He frowns, but he laughs at the same time. "Sergeant!" he cries. "More beer!"

I manage to drink my first bottle and finagle my way out of any more, sure he will call my manhood into question once again for not being at least a two-bottle man, but Muhammed is busy talking to the women. Inga has downed two glasses, and Olive is working on her first glass, but she firmly refuses to have any more.

"We have to be at work early tomorrow morning," she says, and that opens the way for us to excuse ourselves.

"Bring a case of Star for these good people," he says. He turns to us. "Take some beer back for the doctor. And tell him to come next time." It is more of a command than a social comment.

We all assure him that we will pass the word.

✦ ✦ ✦

We had been told about cutting the kola nut, a ritual performed when visiting an Ibo household. In some areas, the host cuts the kola, carefully prying it apart; in others, it is the guest. I was visiting a government official in the area when his wife brought out a small plate with a kola and a knife. I wait. Finally, he waved his hand. "Cut the kola," he said.

I was embarrassed, although he did not seem to mind. Perhaps I should have asked which of us was to do this. I thought I performed it clumsily, but the task was done and I offered him his own kola. We chewed on our pieces, slowly, talking about when we thought secession would occur. It had stopped being an "if" and had become a "when."

✦ ✦ ✦

On our way back, buoyed by the beer and shaken by the anti-aircraft display, we begin to sing spirituals and folk songs, trying to teach Inga the words to some of them. Neither Olive nor I seem to know more than the first verse of anything. Finally, we resort to Christmas carols, and Inga actually joins in on a couple. We finish the second verse of "Adeste, Fideles" just as we pull up behind our house. The lights are on downstairs, but Brace is in bed.

We smoked a lot at Col. Muhammed's and I am sure I'll feel awful in the morning. But, to finish off the evening, I have one more cigarette while I sit cross-legged in my wooden chair and stare out the window.

A plane goes overhead. I aim my cigarette at it and go pow-pow-pow very softly.

APRIL 1969 – ROME

Rome is yellow and orange. When the evening sun covers the buildings in front of me, splashing them with its brilliance, I stop and stare and am struck dumb. Impatient passersby bump me and say things in Italian I probably don't want translated.

Tonight I am going to the opera. Verdi's *Macbeth*. In my new suit, new shoes, new shirt, new tie, new trench coat, even new underwear and socks. And handkerchief. I will head down the stairs of the *pensione* and walk the few blocks to the opera house. I have never had a suit as fine as this one, a dark blue with lining even in the sleeves, and it only cost me 30-some dollars.

From my window, I see the traffic and that glorious sun drenching the far side of the street. This building's four-story shadow is snuggled up against a yellowish-brown building.

✜ ✜ ✜

My farewell to Africa was a glorious early-morning view of the Nile delta from the airplane carrying me from Cairo to Rome. It stunned me how much it *looked* like the Nile delta on all those maps I had seen for so many years! There it was, reaching out farther and farther into the Mediterranean.

The Cessna from Port Harcourt had also taken me west to Lagos on just such a beautiful, clear morning, rising us above the Red Cross vehicles, the long lines of the clinics, the sounds of gunfire as the war went on. For me, it was time to go home. Time to leave a continent I had known for nearly three years. Part of that time had been spent in the classroom, discussing verbs and paragraphs. And part of that time, the unexpected part, had been spent force-feeding medicine down the throats of almost-dead children, one after the other, for months.

And now, after a short time in Europe, I will go home, glad to see family and friends, glad to have familiar foods, to see the leaves of next autumn, but never being able to understand, truly and fully understand, the experience thrust upon me. I feel guilty about leaving, wondering if I should have stayed to work in the clinics, but deciding, at last, that I am tired and will allow myself to be selfish enough to depart, promising myself that I will return, hoping it will be to a peacetime Nigeria.

✦ ✦ ✦

I hand a huge pile of old clothes to the little boy whose father runs this *pensione*. Even my shoes I give him. And the old suitcase I bought in Malawi. Well, not so old, but certainly used and abused and now replaced by a new one I saw in a shop window a couple of streets over. The boy, who is probably 10 years old, can't understand that I want to throw everything away. "Yes, yes," I say, and smile. "*Si, si.*"

I force them back into the box I am using for a wastebasket. When he finally understands, he throws up his hands and says, "*Mama mia!*" and then he goes on in Italian I probably don't want translated.

✦ ✦ ✦

I stare at the black people on the street. I stare so much they give me hostile looks in exchange and I am shaken back to reality. Amid the thousands and thousands of white and light-brown faces, the black ones are startling. And I am sure I know them all. Just sure. They look like people I know, people I knew in Africa during the past three years.

I go into the American Embassy and come up to two black guards at the front desk. Why, I wonder, do they import Africans to work here when they could employ Italians, if they won't bring over Americans? In the middle of my deep frown, one of them says to me, "Hey, how ya doin'? Can we help you?"

I bite my lip to keep from speaking out. I almost say, "What the hell—you're Americans!" How could I explain away that one?

✛ ✛ ✛

I go to mass at St. Peter's. I cannot believe the enormity of the church. The crowds are loud, rude, shoving against one another, and, despite the printed notices that we are not to take photos, they are taking photos by the thousands.

"Get out of the fuckin' way!" screams one American girl from a Catholic-high-school group. She wants some old woman to move so she can get the Pope's picture—he is being carried in a sedan chair. The woman is confused. It is too noisy for her. I am so disillusioned. I try to leave, but the doors are locked. We can't get out. Then, when it's all over, and all the screaming and photo-taking and "fuck you's" are said, everyone runs for the now-unlocked exits and I am carried off my feet right towards a monstrous pillar that has withstood thousands of these crowds (and probably saw smashed against it a lot of innocents). Luckily, just before I am to hit it, I get dropped to the floor and manage to move to the side.

✛ ✛ ✛

The shadows of the building have lengthened themselves as high as the rooftop. The sun is even more brilliant and now I can't see the windows in the next building. Instead, as if each were a star determined to outshine its neighbors, they flash their sunlight back at us. It makes me squint.

✛ ✛ ✛

I feel as if I have washed the dust of Africa off me, particularly now that I have some new clothes and have gotten rid of the old ones. Some of them I had taken with me to Nigeria in 1966.

✦ ✦ ✦

I am living on borrowed peace, sitting on the wide window ledge, having a fine Benson & Hedges, looking at shadows and sunlight and hearing some beautiful music from someone's radio somewhere a couple floors down. Chopin? I think so. The same Chopin who pushed my decision to the forefront and got me into the whole messy war. Do I thank him for that or condemn him? I can't decide. I light another cigarette and listen to the next classical piece.

I enjoy blowing the smoke out of the open window, watching it slowly drift into the light-blue sky.

✦ ✦ ✦

Macbeth. I remember the basic plot so I suppose I'll enjoy this one more than most operas I could have seen. It's a pity I have to go alone.

Is Macbeth Nigerian or Biafran? Power corrupts. Killing and killing and killing, and having it all end in naught. Murder begetting murder. Definitely Modern West African.

"All my pretty ones?" That line I do remember. Maybe Nigeria and Biafra could adopt that as their joint slogan. All the Macduffs who discover their families are gone, in one fell swoop. All my pretty ones. Poof.

✦ ✦ ✦

The sun is fading some now. I should be going soon so I can walk the streets and pause to soak in the flavor. Borrowed peace it is.

There is a knock. It is the boy's father.

"Yes?"

"The boy was worried. Did you wish to dispose of all those things?"

I smile. Mama mia. "Yes, I did. I've just come from Africa where I was for a few years, and I bought these new clothes—" I gesture at myself.

He smiles. "Of course. Africa. Of course."

"I have some photos. Let me show you." The shop developed them for me in only two days. And I didn't have to wait in line. Miracles.

I pull the prints out of my pocket. "This is a clinic where I was working."

"Biafra?" he asks. Everyone knows about Biafra. I almost say yes, it would be easier to say yes, but I say no, it is Nigeria.

"Nigeria. The same."

"The same war, yes. I was on the other side."

"A doctor?"

"Me? No, I helped with medicine and food, though."

The next several pictures are of the others: Olive clowning on the front porch; Inga holding the scruffy little bush we used for a Christmas tree; Brace cutting my hair. I explain who they are. Then we come to the photos of the children. I explain the diseases, even the names of some of the children that I surprise myself by remembering. Thankgod. Ozuzu. Charity.

The man shakes his head. "I saw that in the war."

"The war?"

"World War the Second. I saw that." He pushes the photos towards me.

"But I have more. Here are some of the other children—"

"You are sure you don't want any of those clothes?" He says 'clothe-ez.'

"I'm sure, but—"

"Good-bye. Go out and enjoy Rome. The Eternal city. Go to the Vatican. Go see our Papa."

"I did." He doesn't hear me.

"Go to the Colosseum. The old Romans." He is closing the door, my own door, on me. "Go to the Forum. Enjoy the Forum. Enjoy Rome." He shuts the door.

I look down at the photos in front of me, the faces of Olive and Brace and Inga looking up at me, expectantly, waiting for me to shoot another one, waiting for me to get in the Land Rover and go somewhere, waiting for me to read my scripture and jerk my head down obediently for my silent portion of the prayer ritual. And, without meaning to, I push them aside like so many new playing cards rubbing slickly against one another, and get to the children.

They show no such expectations. They stare off-camera right and off-camera left. One of them is held up by an interpreter. It stares right at the camera, right into the camera, right through the camera.

In the next photo, the same two are there; this time, the interpreter is looking with a smile at the child and gesturing at the camera. This shot is off-camera right.

I sit down heavily on the bed, right on top of my new trench coat, and spread the photos out before me, fanning them out. Suddenly, finally, I feel it begin to well up inside me, building and building toward a release.

Determined to be left alone, I hold in my sobs, forcing my chin down against my chest, and clutch both hands against the back of my neck. I grab the pillow and bury my face in it.

I go on like this for a very long time until I simply cannot do it anymore.

Finally, I put down the pillow, collect the photos and put them in my suitcase, wrapping them in a shirt.

I wash my face and leave for the opera.

THE END

Epilogue

JANUARY 1970 – CALUMET CITY, ILLINOIS

SURRENDER

biafra surrendered
she shouted over the phone
ringing and the clump
of notepads and bookstore order forms

one of those people who likes to bring
you good news and who loves
to bring you bad

frozen in time is an orange art book
just in my vision
picasso perhaps
or maybe miro
and the stopped blur
of it all is only contrasted
to her face telling the news
and harsh ground noise
of people returning
xmas gifts
they read and fingered and wanted to exchange

biafra surrendered
she told me
knowing that I was
the prime person
to tell
one of the few
in the whole seamy south side
of chicago who could find it
on a map

biafra:
memories of children lying
on their agbadas
reading books
in the library
and old toothless women
pans of yams on their heads
smiling at me
and offering greetings
I did and did not understand
as we met along the sort of paved road at dusk

memories of trenches being dug
on the school grounds
and being interrogated by huffy fat police
for daring to want to take
an innocent picture

memories of carrying too much later
a dead baby
light as a piece of styrofoam

red cross land rovers
stopping at black roadblocks
my standing white arms up
in my own headlights
a display for them all
but luckily never a target

dancing to a frenzied band
and cheers of wide eyed villagers

dancing with an old man
both of us keeping the beat
with our hips and
clapping our hands
as the crowd went wild
never having seen a white man walk before
let alone deign to come into their
mud walled communal house
to shake his rhythmic hips
getting back to the soil
in a continent he did not realize
until then that he owed some heritage to

and the image of her
poised
the news on her lips
the phones ringing
the orange art book
on the shelf
is the final picture
of that war all at once remembered
in a bookstore near chicago
the day biafra died

ABOUT THE AUTHOR

John Sherman lived in Africa for several years in the 1960s and 1970s. Between 1966 and 1969, he was a Peace Corps Volunteer teacher in Nigeria and Malawi and a relief worker with the International Committee of the Red Cross in Nigeria. Upon his return to Africa in 1971, he worked at the office of Peace Corps/Ghana in Accra, while serving as national director of the American Field Service. He was also a graduate student at the University of Ghana, taking courses in African Studies (Literature). He later served as a teacher in Zaire before moving back to the U.S. in 1975.

In the United States, he has frequently published articles and lectured on current affairs in Africa and on his own experiences on that continent.

Sherman's third book of poetry, *Marjorie Main: Rural Documentary Poetry* (Mesa Verde Press, 1999), is a collection of poems about growing up on a farm in Indiana in the 1940s and 1950s. A manuscript that included most of the poems that appear in *Marjorie Main* earned him a Finalist position in the Walt Whitman Award competition sponsored by the Academy of American Poets.

An earlier poetry book, *America Is A Negro Child: Race Poems* (Mesa Verde Press, 1981), illustrated by S.M. Lurie, includes poems that draw upon his experiences living in Africa and his views on America's—and his own—struggle with race.

Researching and writing *Santa Fe: A Pictorial History* (Donning, 1983 and 1996) and *Taos: A Pictorial History* (Gannon, 1990) gave Sherman ample opportunities to indulge his love for history and photography. He received the New Mexico Governor's Award of Honor in 1985 for Historic Preservation for his book on Santa Fe.

He has also published poetry in many literary magazines and anthologies and numerous feature articles and photos in major newspapers around the U.S.

His weekly humor column, "Generally Sherman," appeared in *The Santa Fe Reporter* for six years and was later a daily feature on a Santa Fe radio station.

Sherman now owns a public relations and marketing firm in Indianapolis. He continues to write freelance articles on a variety of subjects.

He received an Individual Artist Grant from the Indiana Arts Commission in 2000 to help fund readings of his poetry in Indiana high schools. He frequently participates in poetry readings and has won several prizes for his poetry.

He received a second Individual Artist Grant in 2002 to promote *War Stories*.